Signaling lifeguard, Ocean City, Maryland

National Geographic's
Driving Guides to America
Washington, D.C.
And Virginia, West Virginia, Maryland, and Delaware
By K. M. Kostyal
Photographed by
Richard Nowitz
and Pete Souza
Prepared by
The Book Division
National Geographic Society
Washington, D.C.

Credits

National Geographic's Driving Guides To America Washington, D.C., and Virginia, West Virginia, Maryland, and Delaware

By K.M. Kostyal
Photographed by Richard Nowitz *and* Pete Souza

Published by
The National Geographic Society

Reg Murphy
President and Chief Executive Officer
Gilbert M. Grosvenor
Chairman of the Board
Nina D. Hoffman
Senior Vice President

Prepared by The Book Division

William R. Gray
Vice President and Director
Charles Kogod
Assistant Director
Barbara A. Payne
Editorial Director

Driving Guides to America

Elizabeth L. Newhouse
Director of Travel Books and Series Editor
Cinda Rose
Art Director
Thomas B. Powell III
Illustrations Editor
Caroline Hickey, Barbara A. Noe
Senior Researchers
Carl Mehler
Map Editor and Designer

Staff for this book

Barbara A. Noe
Project Manager
Mary Luders
Text Editor
Joan Wolbier
Designer
Thomas B. Powell III
Illustrations Editor
Carl Mehler
Map Editor and Designer

Sean M. Groom
Michael H. Higgins
Keith R. Moore
Shana E. Vickers
Researchers

Paulette L. Claus
Copy Editor

Thomas L. Gray, Joseph F. Ochlak, Tracey M. Wood
Map Researchers
Tracey M. Wood and Mapping Specialists, Inc.
Map Production
Tibor G. Tóth
Map Relief

Meredith C. Wilcox
Illustrations Assistant
Richard S. Wain
Production Project Manager
Lewis R. Bassford, Lyle Rosbotham
Production

Rhonda J. Brown, Kevin G. Craig, Dale M. Herring, Peggy J. Purdy
Staff Assistants

Rick Davis
Indexer

Thomas B. Blabey, Mary E. Jennings, Dean Nadalin
Contributors

Manufacturing and Quality Management

George V. White, *Director*
John T. Dunn, *Associate Director*
Vincent P. Ryan, *Manager*

Desk at Berkeley Plantation, Virginia

Cover: Jefferson Memorial, Washington, D.C.
Ken Sherman/Graphistock

Previous pages: Lincoln Memorial and Memorial Bridge across the Potomac River, Washington, D.C.

Facing page: Shenandoah Valley, near Stanley, Virginia

Library of Congress CIP data: page 160

Contents

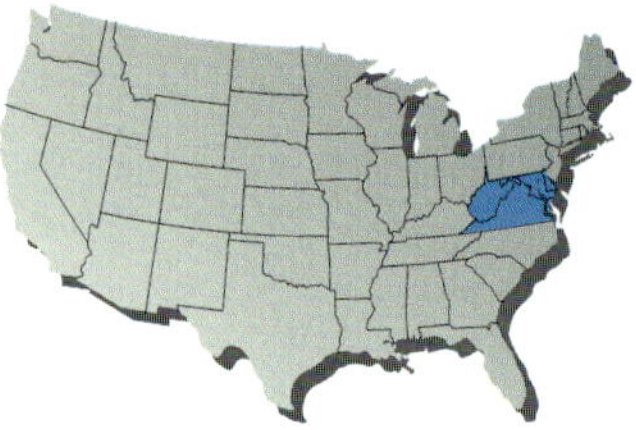

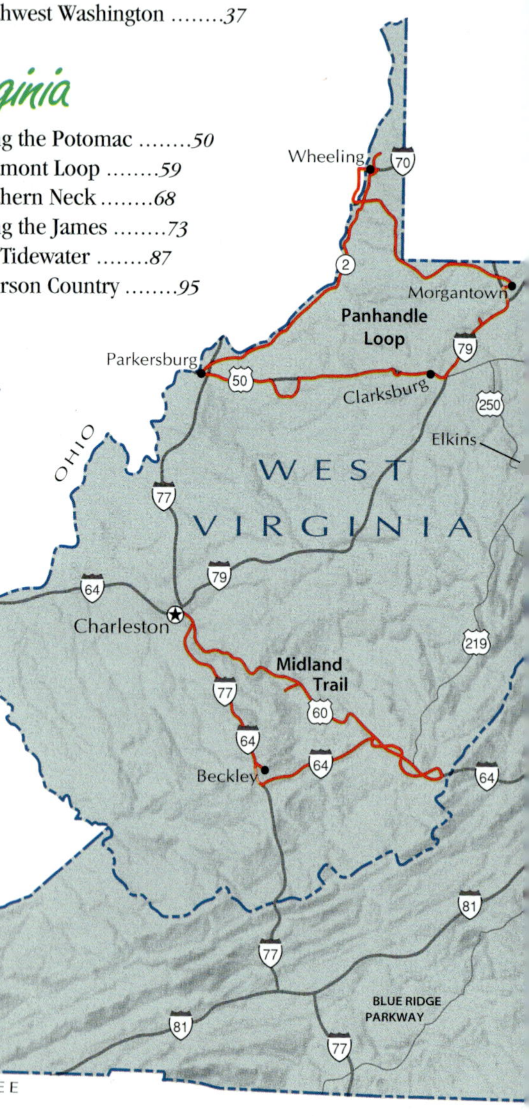

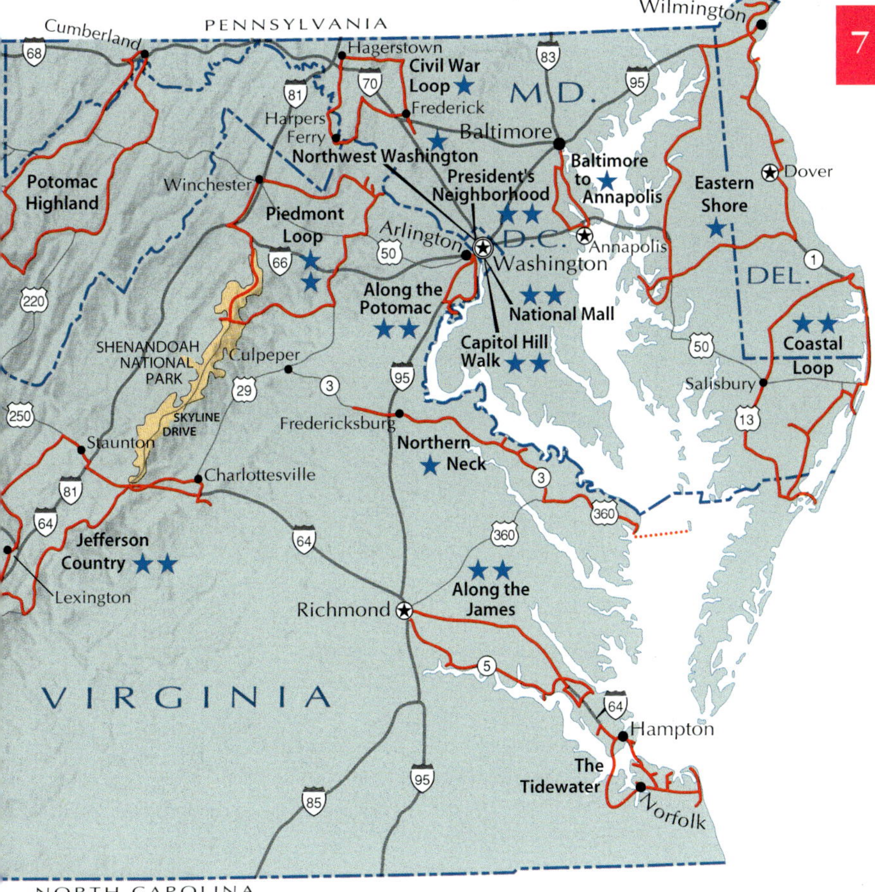

PENNSYLVANIA
Cumberland
Hagerstown
Civil War Loop
Frederick
M.D.
Wilmington
Baltimore
Harpers Ferry
Northwest Washington
President's Neighborhood
Baltimore to Annapolis
Eastern Shore
Dover
Potomac Highland
Winchester
Piedmont Loop
Arlington
D.C.
Washington
Annapolis
DEL.
Along the Potomac
National Mall
Capitol Hill Walk
Coastal Loop
SHENANDOAH NATIONAL PARK
Culpeper
SKYLINE DRIVE
Salisbury
Fredericksburg
Northern Neck
Staunton
Charlottesville
Jefferson Country
Lexington
Along the James
Richmond
VIRGINIA
Hampton
The Tidewater
Norfolk
NORTH CAROLINA
68
81
70
83
95
220
66
50
29
3
250
64
360
13
1
5
85

Reconsidering History

I grew up in the low languid tidelands of Virginia, where the air was heavy with the smell of salt marshes, and wide soft sandbars would emerge like mirages from the sea as the moon tugged on the tides. Walking across those saltwater flats, looking for soft crabs or gar fish or whatever else might wriggle across our paths, we kids would sometimes spot a half-exposed arrowhead or tomahawk, and we'd yank it greedily from the sand to add to our desk-drawer collections. We were not overly impressed with the long history, or prehistory, of those things, because history, after all, was all around us. Our class trips were to Jamestown and Williamsburg, Richmond and Washington, whose white-marble temples of government silenced even us. At our local town parades, we watched history in the making as the country's first astronauts—Shepherd, Grissom, Glenn, and the others training at Langley—sat in open cars and waved to us, their neighbors. History past, history in the making—so prevalent as to go almost unnoticed.

Dolly Sods Wilderness, Pendleton County, West Virginia

But age has a way of engendering a respect for history, and now I walk this stretch of the East Coast with a more considered step, knowing that it has witnessed as much history as any spot on the continent. Each grand Georgian manor, each chinked cabin, each monumental Washington building has a humanness to it, is a testament to the struggles, visions, fortitude of real people—people whose lives and dreams in the end were not so very different from our own.

Whether you are strolling the streets of the nation's Capital, roaming the mountains of Appalachia, dipping through the pleated hills of horse country, or cruising the shallow chop of the Chesapeake Bay, you can be sure history will be your constant companion in this part of the country. In your travels, maybe you'll be lucky enough to spot one of those half-revealed arrowheads, or glimpse the morning mist billowing across a battlefield, or catch some other whisper of past lives and times that will make your own life and time a little richer.

K. M. Kostyal

About the Guides

NATIONAL GEOGRAPHIC'S DRIVING GUIDES TO AMERICA invite you on memorable road trips through the United States and Canada. Intended both as travel planners and companions, each volume guides you on preplanned tours over a wide variety of terrain to the best places to see and things to do. The authors, expert regional travel writers, star-rate (from none to two ★★) the drives and points of interest to make sure you don't miss their favorites.

All distances and drive times are approximate (if you linger, as you should, plan on considerably more time). Recommended seasons are the best times to go, but roads and sites are open all year unless otherwise noted. Besides the stated days of operation, many sites close on national holidays. For the most up-to-date site information, it's best to call ahead when possible.

Then, with this book and a road map, set off on your adventure through this awesomely beautiful land.

Sailboat at Chesapeake Bay Maritime Museum, St. Michaels, Maryland

MAP KEY and ABBREVIATIONS

National Battlefield
National Battlefield Park .... N.B.P.
National Historical Park .... N.H.P.
National Military Park .... N.M.P.
National Park .... N.P.
National River
National Seashore
U.S. Military Facility

City Park
National Cemetery
National Forest .... NAT. FOR., N.F.
National Recreation Area .... NAT. REC. AREA
State Forest .... S.F.

National Wildlife Refuge .... N.W.R.

Local Park
State Park .... S.P.

ADDITIONAL ABBREVIATIONS

B & O	*Baltimore and Ohio*
C & D	*Chesapeake and Delaware*
C & O	*Chesapeake and Ohio*
Cr.	*Creek*
FRWY.	*Freeway*
HIST.	*Historic*
H.S.P.	*Historical State Park*
HWY.	*Highway*
MEM. MUS.	*Memorial Museum*
Mt.-s	*Mount, Mountain-s*
MUS.	*Museum*
NAT.	*National*
NAT. MON.	*National Monument*
NAT. MUS.	*National Museum*
N. Br.	*North Branch*
N. Fk.	*North Fork*
PKWY.	*Parkway*
S. Fk.	*South Fork*
W. Fk.	*West Fork*

Featured Drive
Interstate Highway (95)
U.S. Federal Highway (50)
State Road (20)
County or Local Road (606)
Trail
State or National Border
Ferry
Canal
Forest Boundary

■ Point of Interest
National Capital
State Capital
Dam = Falls
) (Gap
M Metro Station (subway)

POPULATION

● **Baltimore**	500,000 and over
● Norfolk	50,000 to under 500,000
● Dover	under 50,000

A Short History of the Capital

When America gained its independence from Britain, the founding fathers were faced with binding 13 disparate colonies into a nation. As a gesture of unity, they wanted to establish a federal city that would serve as both the administrative and symbolic heart of a central government. For almost a decade, Congress moved between such major cities as New York and Philadelphia, all angling to become the permanent seat of power.

In 1790 Congress empowered President Washington to choose a permanent site. After some deliberation, he selected an area on the Potomac about 16 miles upstream from his own Mount Vernon. It encompassed the Virginia port of Alexandria and the virtually undeveloped land across the water, at the confluence of the Potomac and Anacostia Rivers. By congressional decree, all federal buildings were to be developed on that distant side of the Potomac.

To coax a city out of the tidal marshlands, Washington chose an aggressive but visionary French architect who had fought in the Revolution. Pierre L'Enfant was in his early 30s when he arrived in Georgetown in the spring of 1791, ready to create for the new country a city worthy of its magnificent new ideals. Choosing the high ground of Jenkins Hill as the location of the "Congress House," he envisioned a grand avenue radiating out from it, ending with an equestrian statue of Washington. On a north-south axis to that statue, he placed the "President's House." The problem of Tiber Creek, which ran through this area, would be overcome by the use of canals, turning it into a watercourse with fountains and reflecting pools.

Surrounding this ceremonial public area, L'Enfant planned a grid of streets cut by broad, diagonal avenues punctuated by "roundpoints" (the traffic circles that now flummox visitors and residents alike). Aside from serving as neighborhood parks, these points would also have defensive functions, guarding approaches to the city from all sides.

L'Enfant's flamboyant baroque design, based loosely on the extravagant plan of Versailles, proved a bit overly ambitious for a fledgling country with few skilled artisans, little means of transporting building materials, and modest federal coffers. In less than a year, the obstreperous Frenchman was dismissed. But his vision, if somewhat tempered, remained.

Throughout the 1790s construction eked along on the Capitol Building crowning Jenkins Hill and on the

Tourists in front of the White House

President's House. Thomas Jefferson, an amateur architect himself, became involved in planning the city, and George Washington closely oversaw developments as well, keenly aware that Congress had given him until 1800 to produce a federal city.

In November of that year, the capital was officially relocated from Philadelphia to the still incomplete buildings on the shores of the Potomac. Congressmen groused about life in a frontier town with no civilizing grace. More than one of them lobbied to abandon the place and choose an existing city as capital. But the voices of hope prevailed, and over the next century Washington, D.C., as it became officially designated, slowly assumed the appearance of a city.

Lincoln Memorial, Washington Monument, and Capitol

In 1901 a Senate-appointed commission began to transform the hodgepodge of monuments and museums that had sprung up haphazardly along L'Enfant's grand avenue into what is now the city's showcase—the National Mall. During the 20th century, more world-renowned structures were built here, and urban renewal along Pennsylvania Avenue has at last given that corridor its own elegance. Today, the governmental city of neoclassic marble buildings, offset by greenswards, fountains, and statuary, is deserving of the title given to promote improvement in America's leading cities—"city beautiful." Still a work in progress, the capital continues to change, becoming more cosmopolitan, more ethnically diverse, and richer in the performing arts. L'Enfant, honored for his efforts with a graveside view on the heights of Arlington House across the river, would no doubt be pleased.

National Mall ★★

● 6 miles ● 2 days ● Year-round

The National Mall stands at the heart of monumental Washington, embodying the ideals of democracy in its gleaming white marble edifices, pools, fountains, and perfect greenswards. The Mall honors this country's most hallowed heroes in memorials and monuments, and its many museums celebrate the arts, histories, and cultures of the world. The Smithsonian Institution exerts the most powerful influence here, with nine different buildings, but other stellar institutions such as the National Gallery of Art, the National Archives, and the United States Holocaust Memorial Museum maintain their own strong presences.

Statue of Abraham Lincoln, Lincoln Memorial

To the west of the Mall stands the ❶ **Lincoln Memorial** ★★ *(23rd St. N.W. 202-426-6841),* immediately recognizable as the building pictured on pennies and five-dollar bills. Inside sits a larger-than-life sculpture by Daniel Chester French of the Great Emancipator, staring pensively toward the Capitol. Built in 1922, the monument's 36 Doric columns represent the states in the Union at the time of Lincoln's death. Many demonstrators have spoken out from these steps, literally "backed" by Lincoln as they faced enormous crowds gathered around the long Reflecting Pool below. In 1963 Martin Luther King, Jr., delivered his "I have a dream..." speech here. Well before that, in 1939, opera singer Marion Anderson gave a groundbreaking concert after being barred from performing at nearby Constitution Hall because of her race. If you stroll around to the Potomac side of the monument, you'll see it faces Memorial Bridge with a long view up to Arlington House, once Robert E. Lee's home. The view is intentional, a symbolic reuniting of North and South.

Northeast of the monument, the **Vietnam Veterans Memorial★★** *(Constitution Gardens at 21st St. and Constitution Ave. 202-426-6841)* makes a moving statement amid the greenery of **Constitution Gardens.** Called simply the Wall, its polished granite surface, really two joined triangles, is inset into a hillside and inscribed with the names of the roughly 58,000 men and women of the American armed forces who were killed or reported missing in action in Vietnam. The 21-year-old Yale architectural student, Maya Ying Lin, who designed the Wall in the early 1980s, said of it, "Take a knife and cut open the earth, and with time the grass would heal it." Judging by the many visitors who come here to mourn or pay hushed respects, Lin's moving symbol of healing remains powerfully affecting.

Vietnam Veterans Memorial

Three other, more conventional, war monuments stand nearby—one to women who served in Vietnam (1993) and another by Frederick Hart depicting soldiers in that same conflict (1984). The latter was commissioned to help abate the controversy that first raged concerning the abstract quality of the Wall. The third, dedicated in 1995, memorializes soldiers who served in the Korean War.

Above rises the 2 **Washington Monument★★** *(15th St. N.W. 202-426-6841),* perhaps the city's—and

How to Negotiate the Capital

As in all big cities, street parking is at a premium in Washington, particularly in the Mall area. However, free public parking spaces with a three-hour limit are available after 10 a.m. along the Mall's Jefferson and Madison Drives. If you arrive right at ten, you stand a good chance of getting a spot. A more convenient way to visit Mall sites is via the commercial **Tourmobile** *(202-554-7950. Fee)*, which runs continuously all day, stopping at the major monuments, museums, and Capitol Hill sites. Your ticket allows you to get on and off as many times as you like. The **Metro** *(202-637-7000)*, Washington's subway system, runs throughout the city and into the suburbs. Though expensive, the Metro offers a one-day, $5 (per rider) tourist pass that allows unlimited rides from 9:30 a.m. to midnight on weekdays and from 8 a.m. to midnight on weekends and holidays. Passes are available at Giant and Safeway stores and at various Metro stations.

country's—quintessential landmark, piercing the Washington skyline with austere marble simplicity. Crowning a small rise near the east end of the Reflecting Pool, this 555.5-foot obelisk was long in the making. As early as 1783, the Continental Congress voted to erect an equestrian monument to Washington. But, perhaps providentially, the new nation could not afford such statements, and for decades the idea languished. Then in 1833, private citizens founded the Washington National Monument Society and raised enough funds to begin planning the memorial. Preeminent architect Robert Mills won the design competition with his "grand circular colonnaded building … from which springs an obelisk." Construction actually got underway in 1848, and over time the concept was simplified to a single shaft. The monument committee solicited aid from states, aid that eventually took the form of granite blocks for the interior, engraved with appropriately respectful inscriptions. When Pope Pius IX contributed a block from a Roman temple, it was stolen by the radical, anti-Catholic "Know-Nothings" of the American Party.

With 150 feet of the obelisk completed, work ceased while the Civil War raged. Construction resumed in 1878, but contracts changed hands, and the marble used was quarried from a different source, resulting in the subtle color differentiations still visible today. That small flaw does not dissuade the crowds that perpetually wrap around the monument beneath fluttering American flags, waiting to ride the elevator to the observation room at its summit. From here, the city and the Virginian suburbs swell below, divided by the sweep of the Potomac.

South of the monument, the quiet waters of the **Tidal Basin** reflect the changing panoply of the seasons. In early spring, the scene becomes an unforgettable mirage of pink, as Japanese cherry trees in full, creamy bloom weep their petals into the basin's waters. The trees have a distinguished lineage, a gift to the city in 1912 from the mayor of Tokyo.

Appropriately, the nation's great gardener and aesthete, Thomas Jefferson, keeps an eye on the scene from the ❸ **Jefferson Memorial** ★★ *(Off Ohio Dr. 202-426-6841)*. Modeled on the Roman Pantheon, it stands at the edge of the Tidal Basin, its domed Ionic colonnade an honor to the third President's love of classical architecture. Like so many neoclassic Washington buildings of the

Bicyclist and strollers along the Tidal Basin

1930s, this was designed by John Russell Pope. In the center of the open-air monument, a bronze Jefferson stands holding a rolled parchment, a symbol of his Declaration of Independence. More of his memorable writings are inscribed on the encircling walls.

From here, walk back toward the city, heading right on the pathway curving up to 14th Street to the **Bureau of Engraving and Printing** *(14th and C Sts. S.W. 202-874-3188. Mon.-Fri. Tours fill quickly April-Sept.).* A break from the high-toned sublimity of the monuments, this printing plant offers a look at just how the nation's paper currency is produced. With its presses running nonstop, the bureau prints billions of dollars in paper money and billions of postage stamps annually. The exact number of bills and their denominations are regulated by the Federal Reserve Board, but normally most of the bills printed here are one-dollar bills, as their heavy use gives them a street life of only 18 months.

The guided tour begins in a processing area where large linen-and-cotton currency sheets are printed with bill impressions. The sheets are then passed into an area where they're examined and trimmed. A third area overprints the Treasury seal, serial numbers, and the Federal

Reserve District seal and number. After this, the sheets are cut into separate bills, stacked, and sent to Federal Reserve banks throughout the country.

Next door rises one of the newest and most visited sites on the Mall—the **United States Holocaust Memorial Museum★★** *(100 Raoul Wallenberg Pl. S.W. 202-488-0400. Passes are necessary only for the permanent exhibit; advance passes through Ticketmaster (fee) 202-432-SEAT or 800-551-SEAT. Free same-day passes available at museum from 10 a.m., but arrive early as they can go quickly).* This recent addition to the Mall was conceived to perpetuate the memory of the victims of the World War II Holocaust. The massive limestone exterior encases an interior courtyard whose redbrick walls are meant to recall the architecture of Nazi death camps such as Auschwitz. Off the courtyard, the emotionally riveting exhibit, "Daniel's Story," traces the life of a young German Jewish boy in the 1940s, from his secure middle-class home to the privations and horrors of the death camps.

Tower of Faces, United States Holocaust Memorial Museum

The museum's darkly powerful permanent exhibit dominates the remainder of the building, with historic footage and artifacts tracing Hitler's rise to power and his increasing obsession with his "final solution" to the problem of Jews and other "impure" races and individuals. In the hushed marble Hall of Remembrance, an eternal flame burns for the more than 11 million victims of the resulting Holocaust.

As you exit the museum, turn left down 14th Street. The massive, turreted redbrick government building just beyond was built in 1879 to house an earlier Bureau of Engraving and Printing. Continue up 14th Street, turning right on Jefferson Drive, where the **Smithsonian Institution★★** *(202-357-2700. All museums free and open daily)* commences a corridor of world-class museums. The concept for the Smithsonian began with English scientist and man of letters James Smithson (1765-1829). Although he never traveled to the United States, he bequeathed his estate to this country's government, stipulating the moneys be used "to found at Washington, under the name of the Smithsonian Institution, an Establishment for the increase and diffusion of knowledge among men." The Smithsonian now ranks as one of America's great cultural achievements and the largest complex of museums in the world. Besides its eight Mall museums (and the Castle), the institution manages two museums in New York, an astrophysical observatory in Massachussetts, numerous scientific research centers throughout the world, and five other sites in D.C.—the National Portrait Gallery, the adjoining National Museum of American Art, the Renwick Gallery, the Anacostia Museum, and the National Zoological Park.

The first you'll encounter on this tour of the Mall is the elegant marble 4 **Freer Gallery** *(12th St. and Jefferson Dr. S.W.)*. Detroit industrialist Charles Lang Freer left his outstanding collection of American and Asian art to the Smithsonian in 1919, also giving the moneys to build this refined Italian Renaissance gallery. Among the museum's extensive collection of works by American artist James McNeill Whistler is his fanciful Peacock Room.

Like the Freer, the **Arthur M. Sackler Gallery** *(1050 Independence Ave. S.W.)* was conceived by an individual. Dr. Sackler, a New York psychiatrist, was a voracious private collector with a connoisseur's eye. In 1982 he donated his superb collection of Asian art to the Smithsonian, and now gallery after gallery is filled with exquisite Chinese jades, Neolithic bronzes, beautifully wrought Near Eastern gold and silver, and a renowned series of Islamic manuscripts that span the 11th through the 19th centuries. The architecture of the museum creates a compelling atmosphere for the collection. A green, pyramidal roof covers an entrance pavilion leading to a cool, winding warren of underground galleries. Viewing the objets d'art in this undistracted subterranean setting seems to intensify their aspect.

A similar pavilion, this one with a rounded roof, stands across the pleasant **Enid A. Haupt Gardens** from the Sackler. This serves as the gateway to another underground museum, paralleling the Sackler in style and connected to

Enid A. Haupt Gardens and the Smithsonian Institution Castle

it by a subterranean corridor: The **National Museum of African Art** *(950 Independence Ave. S.W.)*, which once occupied the Capitol Hill town house of abolitionist leader Frederick Douglass, is dedicated to the study, collection, and exhibition of the arts of Africa. Focusing on traditional African arts from south of the Sahara, the treasures on display range from the detailed artwork of Benin sculptures to the figurative wood works of the Yoruba and Asante peoples, along with masks and sculptural art of many other ethnic groups.

Chokwe Mask, National Museum of African Art

At the rear of the Haupt gardens, flanked by these two museums, stands the Smithsonian's signature building, the aptly named **Smithsonian Castle** *(Mid-Mall on Jefferson Dr.)*, its nine towers rising from a crenellated cornice. A true piece of Romanesque Revival architecture designed by James Renwick, Jr., the red Seneca sandstone Castle opened as the first Smithsonian building in 1855. No longer a museum, it now houses the Institution's management offices as well as a Visitor Center, where touch screens and maps allow tourists to plan their visit to the Smithsonian and other Washington sites.

Next door, the **Arts and Industries Building** *(Mid-Mall on Jefferson Dr.)* offers a nostalgic look at the past. Its 1881 exterior has a Victorian whimsicality in keeping with its purpose: to house a portion of the massive amounts of artifacts left over from the 1876 Centennial Exhibition held in Philadelphia. Today, two of the four wings radiating out from a central fountained and skylit rotunda remain filled with those same artifacts—machinery, gizmos, and exotica celebrating the best the world had to offer in 1876. The other wings house changing exhibits dealing with the culture and history of Native Americans and African Americans.

Leaping from old to new, the adjacent **Hirshhorn Museum and Sculpture Garden** *(Jefferson Dr. at 7th St. S.W.)* celebrates modernity. The distinctive concrete drum-shaped building and its Sculpture Garden contain one of the best collections of modern art in the world. Within, paintings by Edward Hopper, Georgia O'Keeffe, Joan Miró, Piet Mondrian, and abstract expressionists such as Willem de Kooning and Jackson Pollock are represented, as is the challenging contemporary art of Andy Warhol and Jasper Johns. Works by 19th-century American masters and a number of French sculptors can also be found. The museum's benefactor, Joseph Hirshhorn, arrived in Brooklyn early in this century as a poor Latvian émigré. A genius at finance, he became a Wall Street broker at the age of 18 and went on to make a fortune in uranium investments. After his collection was exhibited at New York's Guggenheim Museum in 1962, Hirshhorn was courted by a number of different countries, all offering to establish a museum to house his masterpieces. Persuaded by President Lyndon Johnson and Dillon Ripley, then Secretary of the Smithsonian, Hirshhorn ultimately donated some 12,000 works of art to this museum bearing his name.

"Lunar Bird" by Joan Miró, Hirshhorn Sculpture Garden

Raised on piers, the museum, designed by Gordon Bunshaft, dominates a plaza punctuated with large works by such contemporary sculptors as Claes Oldenburg and Tony Cragg. In front of the museum, facing the Mall, the sunken Sculpture Garden displays classically modern masterworks, including sculpture by Auguste Rodin, Henry Moore, Alexander Calder, and Henri Matisse.

The final Smithsonian building on the east side of the Mall, the **National Air and Space Museum** *(Independence Ave. at 6th St. S.W. Adm. fee for theater and planetarium shows)* celebrates the romance of aviation in both its exhibits and its visitor count. Year after year a steady stream of admirers pours through its doors, making it the most popular museum in the city. Inside the museum's large, sleek facade, the history of flight—and the epic-making flying machines that made it possible—are recounted and preserved in loving detail. The Wright Brothers' 1903 Flyer is here, as is Charles Lindbergh's *Spirit of St. Louis;* the Apollo 11 capsule, whose lunar module landed astronauts on the moon; and a more recent U-2 spy plane. You can experience the thrill of being airborne in the museum's five-story IMAX theater, or peer deep into the heavens at the **Albert Einstein Planetarium.**

1937 Grumman G-21 Goose, Natl. Air and Space Museum

Stroll a couple of blocks toward the Capitol, where a warm tropical air and heady perfumes fill the huge greenhouse that constitutes the 5 **U.S. Botanic Gardens** *(1st St. S.W. and Maryland Ave. 202-225-7099).* Sweet-smelling orchids, banyans, and other exotics mingle here with seasonal floral displays of mums and poinsettias. The lovely **Bartholdi Fountain** dominates a gracious park and pool on the Mall in front of the greenhouse.

Follow Fourth Street across the Mall to its north side, where the polished angles of the breathtaking East Building of the 6 **National Gallery of Art**★★ *(Madison Dr. and 4th St. N.W. 202-737-4215)* glint in the sunlight. I. M. Pei designed this monumental building on a trapezoidal site, to make an architectural statement that would simultaneously contain the boldness of modern art, serve as a showpiece for the northeast corner of the Mall, and harmonize with the classical architecture of the adjacent West Building. As with the older West Building, it was largely the Pittsburgh steel fortune of financier and statesman Andrew Mellon that bankrolled this new structure.

Even the plaza linking the two buildings does not suffer from understatement. Seven glass tetrahedrons protrude from its rough stone surface, and water ripples down a waterslide. At the museum entrance, an organic rounded form, unmistakably by 20th-century British sculptor Henry Moore, makes clear that this is a place of masterpieces. Inside, the museum's cavernous skylit atrium sweeps upward, showcasing an immense mobile by Alexander Calder. Intimate galleries off this main space feature rotating exhibits of smaller works. Other exhibit spaces angle off the museum's three levels, highlighting 20th-century painting and sculpture as well as major traveling and special exhibitions. An underground concourse, with more exhibits, a café, cafeteria, and bookstore, links the East and West Buildings.

The severe neoclassic lines of the original National Gallery, now called the West Building, are the work of John Russell Pope. The museum's Tennessee marble facade extends 785 feet (from Fourth to Seventh Streets), making it one of the largest marble buildings in the world. Chartered by Congress in 1937, the museum was the brainchild of Andrew Mellon. Early in his life, Mellon began collecting European art, often traveling to the Continent for that purpose with his friend Henry Clay Frick, who gave New York its famous Frick Collection. During his tenure as Secretary of the Treasury in the 1920s, Mellon hit upon his plan to endow a national gallery of art. In the next decade, he collected ardently, focusing on the true masterpieces of Western art, including a score of superb pieces he acquired from Leningrad's Hermitage Museum. In 1941 his long dreamed of National Gallery of Art opened. With its healthy endowments, it has continued to grow and now stands as one of the world's foremost repositories of masterworks.

"The Dancer" by Renoir, National Gallery of Art

Beneath the high dome of the West Building's rotunda, a bronze statue of Mercury wings his way above a fountain surrounded by dark Italian marble columns. Two stately corridors lined with sculpture sweep off either side of the rotunda, leading to a suite of galleries arranged by country. The galleries west of the rotunda begin with Byzantine religious art, then progress into the ethereal beauty of Italian Renaissance works by masters like Botticelli and Raphael. The pièce

Viewing the Bill of Rights and the preamble and signature pages of the Constitution, National Archives

de résistance is the portrait of Ginera de' Benci (1474) by Leonardo da Vinci. Other galleries on this side of the museum display flamboyant baroque art and the more somber works of such Spanish painters as El Greco and Velázquez. Flemish and Dutch paintings are also represented, including several Rembrandt masterpieces.

On the other side of the rotunda, the story of Western art continues with a strong dose of 17th-, 18th-, and 19th-century French, British, and American paintings. Highlights here include the romantic portraits of Britain's Thomas Gainsborough and America's Gilbert Stuart, the mystic abstractionism of J. M. W. Turner and Albert Pinkham Ryder, and the controlled brushwork of John Singer Sargent. But the greatest draws are the Impressionist galleries, where you'll find paintings by all the greats—Monet, Renoir, Degas, Cassatt, Gauguin, and others.

Leave the National Gallery from the ground-floor Constitution Avenue entrance and walk northwest a short block to the **National Archives**★★ *(Constitution Ave. bet. 7th and 9th Sts. N.W. 202-501-5000).* Yet another building by John Russell Pope, this pedimented limestone repository houses the nation's most hallowed documents. Its soaring, 75-foot-high rotunda, popularly known as the Shrine, serves as an appropriate backdrop to the three "charters of freedom," displayed on a marble dias: the Declaration of Independence, the preamble and signature pages of the Constitution, and the Bill of Rights. A side case holds the 1297 version of England's Magna Carta, on permanent loan to the archives from its owner, Ross Perot. Though lines perpetually snake past these revered parchments, many visitors come here to avail themselves of the genealogical records stored in the microfilm research room, which is open to the public *(Photo ID required. Closed Sun.)*.

Fronting both the Mall and Constitution Avenue, the Smithsonian's **National Museum of Natural History** *(Madison Dr. bet. 9th and 12th Sts. N.W.)* always echoes with the voices of school groups. They come to ogle the 13-foot-high taxidermied African bush elephant that seems to charge across the rotunda, or the 92-foot-long, life-size model of a blue whale that hangs in the Life in the Sea section. Along with the many creatures—present and prehistoric—featured in this museum are dioramas and murals depicting native cultures worldwide, an insect zoo, moon rocks and meteorites, and the Smithsonian HoloGlobe—a rotating globe of the earth. The new Hall of Geology, Gems, and Minerals will open in 1997, featuring the National Gem Collection and a new display of the renowned Hope Diamond, the largest blue diamond in the world.

Next door, the **National Museum of American History** *(Madison Dr. at 14th St. N.W.)* seems to prove that the Smithsonian is indeed the nation's attic. At this final stop on the Mall, progress, nostalgia, Yankee know-how, and simple patriotism are celebrated in the items on display and the stories that accompany them. The original tattered, age-faded star-spangled banner that inspired Francis Scott Key to write the national anthem is exhibited here, as are vintage cars, railroad memorabilia, First Ladies' gowns, and the unforgettable ruby slippers that took Dorothy home in the 1939 film *The Wizard of Oz.*

African bush elephant, National Museum of Natural History

To return to your starting point at the Lincoln Memorial, you can turn left on Constitution Avenue and continue down to 23rd Street. If you are planning to use the subway system, a Metro stop is located almost directly across the Mall, near the Freer Gallery.

President's Neighborhood★★

● 2 miles ● 1 day ● Year-round

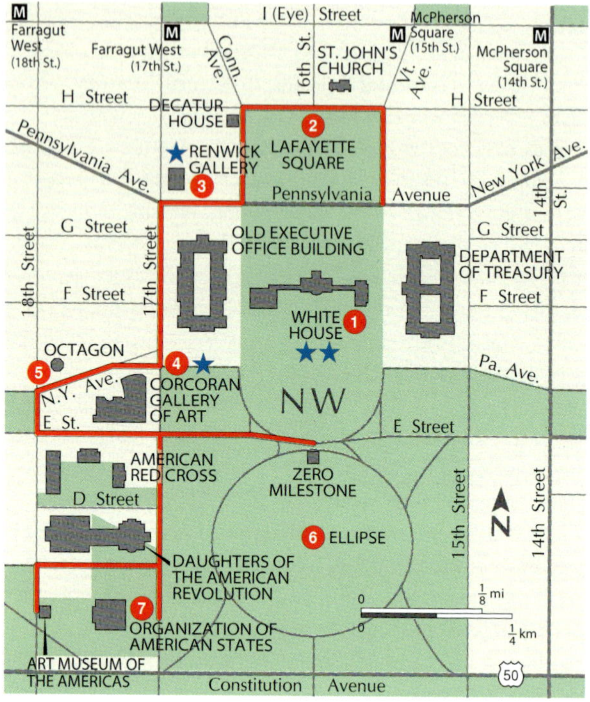

These days, Presidents in office rarely have the opportunity to enjoy their own neighborhood, although the streets around the White House abound with possibilities. Many travelers, too, focus their attention on the home of the First Family and miss the superb museums and historic spots that lie just a block or two away.

Blue Room, the White House

This walking tour begins at the ❶ **White House★★** *(1600 Pennsylvania Ave. 202-456-7041. A Visitor Center at 15th St. near E St. N.W. has exhibits on the White House and issues free, same-day tickets on a first-come, first-served basis, beginning at 7:30 a.m. Tues.-Sat. Or reserve tickets for guided tours by contacting your congressional office at least 8 to 10 weeks in advance).* Aptly named, the white sandstone mansion rises radiantly amid 18 acres of gardens, lawns, and aged shade trees. Its interior possesses a befittingly American character. Making no pretense to palatial ostentation, the rooms are livably proportioned. Thanks to First Lady Jacqueline Kennedy and the preservationists who succeeded her, the house is furnished with an enviable collection of Americana, but it took a century and a half for the President's home to achieve its current form. The original two-story core was designed in the 1790s by a young Irish builder named James Hoban. As with the Capitol, lack of funds and skilled artisans delayed work on it, and it was not until 1800 that the second President, John Adams, was able to move into the partially completed structure. He laid his own private benediction on the house, writing, "May

The White House at dusk

none but honest and wise men rule under this roof." His successor, Thomas Jefferson, moved in and began in his characteristic way to tinker with the building's design. With the help of preeminent architect Benjamin Latrobe, Jefferson drew up plans for colonnaded wings on either side.

In its long illustrious lifetime, the White House has endured fire (set by the British during the War of 1812), neglect, and the sometimes hapless tastes of its occupants. Through it all, it has continued to evolve, taking on a south portico, an east and west wing, a porte cochere, and an ever growing mystique. Every morning visitors enthusiastically queue up to tour the place where the U.S. President lives. The tour snakes through a glass colonnade over-

Vigil at Lafayette Square, across from the White House

looking the Jacqueline Kennedy Garden and on into the small, ground-floor library and Vermeil Room, so named for the French and English gilded silver it contains.

Most of the public reception rooms lie a floor up. The capacious East Room, with its elaborately decorated ceiling and glistening cut-glass chandeliers, serves as a venue for concerts and ceremonies. George Washington surveys the scene in the legendary portrait by Gilbert Stuart that Dolley Madison saved during the 1814 conflagration. Three smaller rooms—the Green Room, Blue Room, and Red Room—offer sweeping views out across the gardens and Ellipse. All boast historic presidential portraits and furnishings brought here in the federal period by the early Presidents, particularly the urbane James Monroe, who had a penchant for French Empire pieces. The final room on this floor is the officious gold-and-white State Dining Room, whose side tables rest on massive gilt eagles. At the tour's end, exit through a cross hall hung with the official portraits of America's Presidents.

The north face of the White House fronts Pennsylvania Avenue, now closed to traffic for security reasons, and **2 Lafayette Square.** Demonstrators have long gathered here, waving placards and yelling slogans toward the President's windows. But the rest of the 7-acre square makes a restful haven in the midst of the city's business district. At its center, a likeness of Andrew Jackson sits astride his horse. At each corner a foreign hero is similarly honored with a statue.

Small but illustrious **St. John's Church at Lafayette Square** *(16th and H Sts. N.W. 202-347-8766),* the Church of the Presidents, stands across H Street. According to architect Benjamin Latrobe, who designed the church in 1815, the simple elegance of the cross-shaped structure "made many Washingtonians religious who were not religious before." Though Latrobe's design has been modified over time, the graceful lines of the church remain, as does the dome he positioned at the center of the sanctuary.

Many of the dignified brick town houses flanking Lafayette Square date from the early decades of nationhood, when this was one of the young city's most fashionable neighborhoods. The first home erected on the square, **Decatur House** *(748 Jackson Pl. N.W. 202-842-0920. Tues.-Sun.; adm. fee),* was built by naval hero Stephen Decatur and designed by Latrobe. The house's prestigious past as center of the Washington social scene is reflected in its federal and Victorian decor. The house is a museum property of the National Trust for Historic Preservation.

Walk back to Pennsylvania Avenue where, turning right and looking across the street, you will encounter one of the city's most extravagant buildings—the **Old Executive Office Building** *(Pennsylvania Ave. and 17th St. N.W. 202-395-5895. By guided tour only, Sat. a.m. Advance reservation required).* Completed in 1888, this flamboyant, unabashed granite mound of tiers, windows, and cast-iron chimneys topped by a mansard roof enjoys a widespread reputation as the best surviving example of Second Empire architecture in this country. Because this particular style, imported from France, so prevailed during the Grant Administration, it is sometimes called General Grant style. Inside, the building's grandeur continues in wide, ornate hallways, cast-iron ornamentation, domes, and skylights. Originally an all-purpose office building housing the State, War, and Navy Departments, it is now occupied only by offices associated with the Executive Branch.

Old Executive Office Building

Keep walking down Pennsylvania to the building that actually inspired the Second Empire craze. The redbrick 3 **Renwick Gallery★** *(Pennsylvania Ave. and 17th St. N.W. 202-357-2700),* the first in this style to be completed in the city, was designed in the mid-1800s by James Renwick to hold the art collection

"Dancer with Gazelles" by Paul Manship, Corcoran Gallery of Art

of William Wilson Corcoran. When it opened its doors in 1874, the Corcoran Gallery of Art (as it was then called) was the city's first art gallery. Because it displayed classical sculpture in various states of dishabille, there were separate viewing hours for men and women. The collection outgrew this building by the end of the century, and a new Corcoran opened a few blocks away. Restored to its Victorian grandeur and placed under the Smithsonian Institution, the Renwick today is mainly devoted to exemplary exhibits of contemporary American crafts. But the second-floor Grand Salon re-creates Victorian tastes in a resoundingly plum-colored room, hung with tiered paintings of romantic 19th-century landscapes and portraiture.

To see the current 4 **Corcoran Gallery of Art★** *(17th St. and New York Ave. N.W. 202-639-1700. Closed Tues.; donation),* walk a few blocks down 17th Street. The distinctive beaux arts building, with its copper roof and central atrium, contains a premier collection of American art. The holdings range from the colonial period through the Hudson River School works of Frederic Church and Albert Bierstadt, to the late 19th- and early 20th-century paintings of Winslow Homer, John Singer Sargent, and Mary Cassatt, and on to the work of contemporary artists. The museum also showcases European fine and decorative arts from the 14th through the 19th centuries.

A block down New York Avenue, the old brick 5 **Octagon** *(1799 New York Ave. 202-638-3105. Tues.-Sun.; adm. fee)* has ornamented this corner of the city since 1801. Actually a six-sided home designed by Capitol architect Dr. William Thornton, the Octagon held a prominent status in early Washington society, and the Madisons stayed here after the British burning of the White House during the War of 1812. While residing here, President Madison signed the Treaty of Ghent, bringing the war to an end. The Octagon, currently owned by the American Architectural Foundation, now holds a museum dedicated to architecture, design, and early Washington, D.C., history.

Walk down 18th Street to E Street, turn left, and proceed across 17th Street to the 6 **Ellipse,** a kind of ceremonial playground for the nation. The gigantic National

Federal District, Federal Dilemma

A unique geopolitical entity, Washington is neither a city nor a state, but a district—a designation that has led to no end of confusion and controversy. Following the Civil War, Congress briefly granted the city territorial status, but within several years, bankruptcy threatened and terrritoriality was revoked. Only in 1961, with the passage of the 23rd Amendment, were district residents allowed to vote in presidential elections. In 1974 Congress granted the city "home rule." An elected mayor and city council now run local affairs and can set local taxes, but Congress ultimately controls the budget and the purse strings. And the only District voice raised in Congress is that of one non-voting delegate to the House of Representatives.

Christmas Tree, decorated here annually, is surrounded by smaller trees that represent the 50 states and the territories. The **Zero Milestone** is also located here, making this the starting point for all mileages radiating from the capital city.

Return to 17th Street where, farther down, three venerable institutions overlook the west end of the Ellipse. The American Red Cross maintains its headquarters here, next door to the headquarters of the **Daughters of the American Revolution** (DAR) *(17th and D Sts. N.W. 202-879-3241. Closed Sat.)*. In this imposing beaux arts headquarters, the public is welcome to tour more than 30 period rooms, each conceived and decorated by a different state. A **museum** displays glass, silver, textiles, and other decorative pieces while the library contains a wealth of genealogical information. The adjacent **Constitution Hall** auditorium has long been a major venue for visiting performers.

The marble-and-terra-cotta-roofed 7 **Organization of American States** (OAS) *(17th St. and Constitution Ave. N.W. 202-458-3000. Mon.-Fri.)* makes a compelling endpoint to the tour. With the grace of a Spanish colonial villa, the OAS is fronted by a wide plaza adorned with allegorical sculptures, including one representing North America by Mount Rushmore artist Gutzon Borglum. The building centers around a courtyard fronted with tropical trees and other plants. The upstairs Hall of the Americas boasts Tiffany rock-crystal chandeliers and stained-glass windows. The Aztec Gardens behind the building are punctuated with more sculpture. At their edge, the **Art Museum of the Americas** *(202-458-6016. Tues.-Sat.)* mounts varying rotating exhibits focusing on Latin America and the Caribbean, along with displays from its extensive permanent collection.

Relaxing in Lafayette Square

Capitol Hill Walk★★

● 2.2 miles ● 1 day ● Year-round

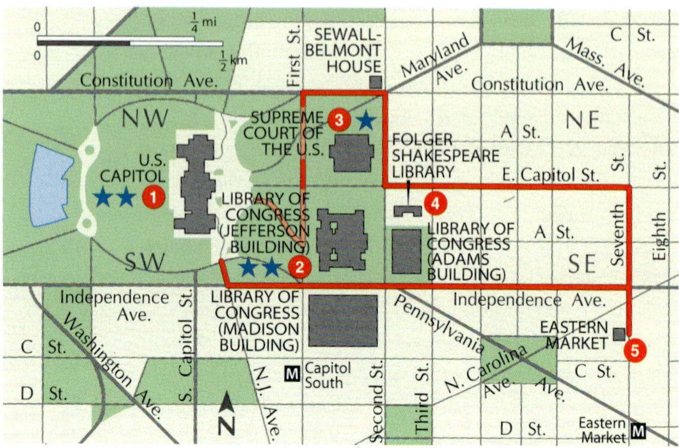

The grand governmental buildings clustered on Capitol Hill, their inhabitants devoted to making and upholding the laws of the land, form the seat of democracy in the United States. The fine art of the U.S. Capitol itself serves as a backdrop to the art of politics, as congressmen and senators sweep along the corridors and lobbyists lurk in the labyrinthine building's many corners. A far more sedate tone prevails in the hushed marble surroundings of the Supreme Court and in those of its neighbor, the Library of Congress. The tour also visits another renowned library—the Folger Shakespeare Library—before ambling past the 19th-century row houses that dignify Capitol Hill's residential streets. The walk ends at rambunctious Eastern Market, the city's last remaining open-air style marketplace. On weekends, produce, flower, and craft vendors set up on the sidewalks around the old building, bringing a lively, old-fashioned commercialism to the Hill.

Begin your walking tour of the Hill at the east steps of the ❶ **United States Capitol★★** *(202-225-6827. Guided tours available but not mandatory. Congressional sessions may be visited only by special pass, available through your representative's or senator's offices. Foreign visitors may obtain passes at the House or Senate Appointment Desks. Congress generally recesses in Aug. and again in the fall through late Jan.).* In 1791, when French architect Pierre L'Enfant looked around at the virtual wilderness he was to turn into a magnificent federal city, his sights naturally fell on the high ground then known as Jenkins Hill. "A pedestal waiting for a monument," he declared. The very place to position the "Congress House." From here, he envisioned a grand, mile-long avenue linking the Capitol with the White House, lined with foreign ministries and cultural institutions. The passionate and grandiose young Frenchman lasted less than a year on the job, but his vision, though toned down, still prevails. The Capitol does indeed crown that high point, and from it Pennsylvania Avenue extends toward the White House.

Ever a work in progress, the Capitol took nearly two centuries to achieve its current form, and it may well change again to meet the demands of a growing populace. In 1793 George Washington presided over the laying of the cornerstone with a daylong Masonic ceremony. The original design for the Capitol, executed by amateur architect Dr. William Thornton, called for a building in the style of Rome's Pantheon. Lack of both skilled workers and supplies slowed construction to a crawl, but in 1800 the north wing was completed and housed not only the Senate, but the House of Representatives, Library of Congress, Supreme Court, and District Court. It took a new architect, Benjamin Latrobe, and another seven years to complete the south wing, with only a wooden walkway linking the two. Five years later, during the War of 1812, the British unceremoniously set fire to the American symbol of democracy, along with much of the rest of the city. The arduous process of building began anew.

United States Capitol

When the Civil War struck, the building was yet again undergoing construction and expansion. It became an enormous hospital for Union wounded, but Lincoln insisted that construction continue even in the midst of

Main Reading Room, Thomas Jefferson Building of the Library of Congress

war, as a "sign that we intend the Union shall go on." In 1863 the grand new cast-iron dome was completed, and the statue of "Freedom," in her flowing robes and feathered helmet, was hoisted into place. She has reigned aloft ever since.

That soaring 180-foot-high dome overhangs the heart of the Capitol, the Rotunda. Between 1864 and 1880, the building's Michelangelo, Italian artist Constantino Brumidi, painted the allegorical "Apotheosis of Washington" that ornaments the eye of the dome, as well as part of the frieze depicting 400 years of the nation's history that runs around its base. More history is recounted in the murals decorating the Rotunda at ground level. If that is not inspiration enough, statues of American leaders look out from pedestals around the room and the stunning, 20,000-pound bronze Columbus Doors celebrate events in the life of the explorer.

Off the Rotunda to the south is the original House Chamber, also called the whisper chamber because the acoustics allowed delegates on one side to overhear what delegates across the room were whispering to each other. Now Statuary Hall, the semicircular room features state heroes. Virginia's Robert E. Lee stands here, along with Hawaii's King Kamehameha and California's pioneering Junipero Serra. On the other side of the Rotunda, the Old Senate Chamber contains original furnishings. After the Senate moved to more spacious quarters in 1859, the

Supreme Court held sessions here until 1935, when it moved into its own building across the street.

The Capitol's ground floor is centered around the low, columned Crypt that lies just below the Rotunda. The name is a bit misleading, as it never served as a burial place. It was intended to hold the remains of George Washington, but Congress did not organize his relocation until some 30 years after his death, by which time his family did not wish him moved from his original burial place at Mount Vernon. The Crypt does, however, memorialize another great President with an enormous sculptured head of Abraham Lincoln by Mount Rushmore artist Gutzon Borglum. Borglum intentionally did not add Lincoln's left ear, as a symbol of the President's abbreviated life. A stone embedded in the Crypt floor marks the point from which the city's four quadrants—northwest, northeast, southwest, and southeast—radiate.

To the north of the Crypt, the Old Supreme Court Chamber, with its green felt desktops and low roofs, makes a compellingly intimate space amid the vastness of the Capitol. The Court met here from 1810 to 1859. This Senate side of the Capitol ends with the stunning Brumidi Corridors, whose arched ceilings and walls are filled with scenes painted by Brumidi and more contemporary artists, and set off with intricate Minton-tile mosaics. To the south, on the House side of the Crypt, the Hall of Columns is lined with much of the statuary that was originally intended for Statuary Hall upstairs. (Engineers determined that the upper hall could not structurally bear the weight of so much heroism.) In the intersecting Hall of Capitols, the 20th-century murals of Allyn Cox record the national scene.

The current House and Senate Chambers, both on the second floor of their respective wings, ensure modern comfort with plush carpeting and richly polished wood. In both chambers, the heroes of the past are amply depicted—and frequently invoked.

Exit the Capitol on the ground floor and cross First Street to the 2 **Library of Congress★★** *(1st St. and Independence Ave. S.E. 202-707-8000. Mon.-Sat.).* This exuberant Italian Renaissance masterpiece, known as the Thomas Jefferson Building, opened in 1897 and is now one of three Library of Congress buildings on the Hill. Together they store 110 million items, including 20 million books. The library's origins date from 1800, when Congress

Other Capital Sites

Basilica of the National Shrine of the Immaculate Conception *(4th St. and Michigan Ave. N.E. 202-526-8300)*
Fonda del Sol Visual Arts Center *(2112 R St. N.W. 202-483-2777. Tues.-Sat.; adm. fee)*
J. Edgar Hoover FBI Building *(E St. bet. 9th and 10th Sts. N.W. 202-324-3447)*
Mary McLeod Bethune Council House N.H.S. *(1318 Vermont Ave. N.W. 202-332-1233. Closed weekends; donation)*
Meridian Intl. Center *(1624 Crescent Pl. N.W. 202-939-5568. Wed.-Sun.)*
National Arboretum *(3501 New York Ave. N.E. 202-245-2726)*
National Building Museum *(4th and F Sts. N.W. 202-272-2448)*
National Museum of Women in the Arts *(New York Ave. and 13th St. N.W. 202-783-5000. Donation)*
Smithsonian's Anacostia Museum *(1901 Fort Pl. S.E. 202-357-2700)*
Smithsonian's National Museum of American Art *(8th and G Sts. N.W. 202-357-2700)*
Smithsonian's National Portrait Gallery *(8th and F Sts. N.W. 202-357-2700)*
Smithsonian's National Postal Museum *(Massachusetts Ave. at 1st St. N.E. 202-357-2700)*

decided it needed a research facility of its own and established one in the Capitol. That early collection was destroyed in the fire of 1814, and to replace it Thomas Jefferson agreed to sell his 6,500-volume personal library to Congress. Sadly, it too was ravaged by fire in 1851, and two-thirds of it lost.

By the late 19th century, the congressional book collection had outgrown its Capitol quarters. Funds were appropriated for the current Thomas Jefferson Building. Modeled after the grand libraries of Europe, it is often ranked as the city's most beautiful building. (Currently under renovation, it is scheduled to completely reopen in 1997.) Its massive copper dome, topped by the "torch of learning," rises above a profusion of columns, balustrades, and busts. A sculpture of Neptune cavorting with his rambunctious sea nymphs fronts the building at street level.

"Contemplation of Justice," in the U.S Supreme Court

Massive stone staircases lead up to the main entrance, opening onto the marbled Great Hall. Its swirl of murals, mosaics, sculptures, and vaults make for an endless visual feast. A grand staircase watched over by cherubs sweeps up to a mezzanine, where a visitors gallery overlooks the equally amazing Main Reading Room. Beneath a gilded, coffered dome, stained-glass windows let in tinted sunlight. Quotations about knowledge and learning ring the walls, as do allegorical statues symbolizing such intellectual endeavors as law, poetry, and science. More bronze statues depict eminent historical figures who contributed to knowledge. Below all this lies the main circulation desk, which is ringed by concentric circles of wooden desks. Truly a public library, the room is open to all readers (18 and older), who may request a book for study.

Just a block away stands the nation's gleaming white-marble temple of justice, the ❸ **Supreme Court of the United States★** *(1st and E. Capitol Sts. N.E. 202-479-3211. Mon.-Fri. Tours when court is not hearing oral arguments. Court* *terms run Oct.-April; call for exact hours. Public access to court sessions is on a first-come, first-served basis).* Ascend its broad staircase, flanked by two imposing sculptured figures of justice, and enter a broad hall lined with the busts of chief justices. Ahead lies the famous, richly columned courtroom. The chief justice, surrounded by the eight associate justices, presides here from a raised bench that looks formidably down on proceedings. Since 1935, this room has been the venue for the highest court in the land, whose interpretation of the Constitution sets the national precedent. Justices are appointed by the President, approved by the Senate, and, unless they are impeached by Congress, serve as long as they choose.

On the ground floor of the building, changing exhibits and a film recount various phases and cases in the history of the Court. A larger-than-life statue immortalizes the "great chief justice," John Marshall. An unpretentious, plain-spoken man, Marshall became the fourth chief justice in 1801 and served until 1835. The power of the judiciary was not fully respected when he took over, but that was soon rectified with his 1803 decision in *Marbury* v. *Madison*. This case established the court's authority to declare an act of Congress unconstitutional, asserting the Court's power of judicial review and ensuring the judiciary's full place in the triumvirate balance of power.

A block farther on First Street, turn right on Constitution Avenue where, on your left, stands a remnant of early Washington, the federal-style **Sewall-Belmont House** *(144 Constitution Ave. at 2nd St. N.E. 202-546-3989. Tues.-Sun.).* Built in 1798, it survived centuries and modifications to become one of the oldest structures on the Hill. Secretary of the Treasury Albert Gallatin lived here in the early 1800s, while working on arrangements for the Louisiana Purchase. Now headquarters of the National Woman's Party, the house holds exhibits detailing the suffragist movement.

First folio of Shakespeare, Folger Shakespeare Library

Cross Constitution and walk straight down Second Street, making a left onto East Capitol Street. The private 4 **Folger Shakespeare Library** *(201 E. Capitol St. S.E.*

202-544-7077) claims the largest collection of the Bard's works in the world. They are housed inside an elegant facade whose art deco classicism won for its architect, Paul Phillipe Cret, kudos from many quarters. Scenes from Shakespeare's plays are portrayed in the bas-relief panels below the windows. The library's interior breaks with modernism and re-creates instead a cavernous darkly paneled Tudor Great Hall, where rare books and manuscripts from the 275,000-volume collection are showcased. Among these holdings are 79 of the 240 first editions of Shakespeare's folios known to exist, and the only known copy of his early play, *Titus Andronicus*. That and some 75,000 other pieces in the collection came through the private efforts of former Standard Oil President Henry Clay Folger and his wife, Emily Jordan Folger, lifelong collectors who established and endowed the library in 1932.

Capitol Hill commuter

An elaborate reproduction of an Elizabethan theater occupies the east end of the building, serving as a home for the acclaimed Folger Consort early music ensemble and for lectures, poetry, plays, and literary readings.

From the Folger continue down past the renovated Victorian and federal row houses of East Capitol Street, turning right at Seventh Street. A few blocks farther is the rustic redbrick 5 **Eastern Market** *(7th St. between C St. and North Carolina Ave. S.E.)*. The marketplace has housed meat, poultry, and produce vendors since 1870, and on Saturdays the sidewalks surrounding it are chockablock with stalls selling everything from locally grown vegetables to the jewelry of Azerbaijan. A wonderful flea market takes place on Sundays. Across the way, a block of boutiques and restaurants create a neighborly, café-society ambience.

To return to the Capitol, walk back up Seventh Street to Independence Avenue. Make a left and keep walking. If you are in need of a Metro subway, the Eastern Market stop is located at the corner of Seventh Street and Pennsylvania Avenue.

Northwest Washington★

● 13 miles ● 1 to 2 days ● Year-round

Washington's most fashionable area, the Northwest quadrant, encompasses embassies, private institutions, and some of the city's loveliest neighborhoods. Beginning at the National Geographic Society headquarters, the drive arrows out along gracious Massachusetts Avenue, lined with the private clubs and endless embassies that now occupy the impressive old mansions. Passing the manicured lawns of the Naval Observatory and the Vice

President's official residence, the drive reaches a high point at the magnificent National Cathedral. From there it heads to the National Zoo and the surprising estate of cereal heiress Marjorie Merriweather Post. Weaving through the woodlands of Rock Creek Park, you arrive in Georgetown, where the rich and powerful mix it up with the bohemian and playful in famous city nightspots.

Begin at the 1 **National Geographic Society**★ *(17th and M Sts. N.W. 202-857-7588).* Brainchild of respected Washington lawyer and financier Gardiner Greene Hubbard, the Society was founded in 1888. Its 33 original members included prominent explorers and scientists, many affiliated with Washington's distinguished Cosmos Club. In the 1890s Alexander Graham Bell, Hubbard's son-in-law, took the helm of the organization and opened membership to anyone interested in "a society for the increase and diffusion of geographical knowledge." Bell, too, passed the reins to his son-in-law, Gilbert Grosvenor, under whose editorship NATIONAL GEOGRAPHIC magazine became a unique part of the American journalistic landscape.

Buildings of the National Geographic Society

Explorers Hall, on the ground floor of a modern marble-and-glass edifice designed in the early 1960s by Edward Durrell Stone, commemorates more than a century of Society-sponsored exploration and research. Here visitors can share in the National Geographic adventure with interactive exhibits that explore the planet, its geography, and the Society's long involvement with exploration and photography. The south end of the museum features changing exhibits, ranging from decorative arts and artifacts of other cultures to the uses of water.

Just up the street, the Romanesque **Cathedral of St. Matthew the Apostle** *(1725 Rhode Island Ave. N.W. 202-347-3215)* serves as the seat of the Roman Catholic Archbishop of Washington. John F. Kennedy's funeral Mass was held in the glittering mosaic interior in 1963.

Another block away stands the headquarters of B'nai B'rith International, the oldest Jewish service organization in the world, founded in 1843. On the building's first floor, the **B'nai B'rith Klutznick National Museum** *(1640 Rhode Island Ave. N.W. 202-857-6583. Sun.-Fri.; donation)* features ritual items and archaeological artifacts, as well as exhibits on Judaic heritage and changing displays by contemporary Jewish artists.

Two blocks north, 17th Street intersects Massachusetts Avenue, a corridor of prestigious institutions, most housed in former mansions. These grand beaux arts buildings recall the Gilded Age, when this neighborhood at the northern frontier of the federal city was the swankiest address in town. Anybody who was anyone, from strike-it-rich gold miners to political pundits, constructed their mansions here. Sadly, many fell to the wrecking ball, but some do survive and continue to give the avenue its dignified character.

The 2 **National Trust for Historic Preservation** *(1785 Massachusetts Ave. N.W. 202-673-4000)* maintains its headquarters in an elegant, five-story beaux arts apartment building put up in 1917 by Stanley McCormick, whose father, Cyrus, invented the reaper. So elegant were these surroundings that they suited even Andrew Mellon, founder of the National Gallery of Art. In the 1920s and 1930s he occupied a floor here, its walls hung with many of the masterpieces now found in the National Gallery.

Rimming the southeast side of **Dupont Circle** are two more mansions, now devoted to the exclusive Sulgrave and Washington Clubs. Dupont Circle itself seems a far cry from their formality. Long a gathering place, the circle teems with professionals, street people, locals, and occasional skateboarders. Shooting off to the north and south is Connecticut Avenue, a commercial corridor with browsable boutiques and a plethora of restaurants.

Continue around the circle and up Massachusetts Avenue, soon passing the formidable redbrick **Blaine Mansion** *(2000 Massachusetts Ave. N.W. Private)*. Built in 1881 by James G. Blaine, a founder of the Republican Party, it now ranks as the oldest surviving mansion in the Dupont Circle vicinity. A few blocks south stands another rare old house, the 3 **Heurich Mansion** *(1307 New Hampshire Ave. N.W. 202-785-2068. Wed.-Sat.; adm. fee)*. Its classic late-Victorian exterior is graced with brick-and-brownstone arches, a tower, and a fine porte cochere. Now home to the Historical Society of Washington, D.C., the house preserves its dark, richly formal interior in the lower floors, while the upper floors are devoted to the society's extensive library and historical exhibits. A German brewer named Christian Heurich built the mansion in the 1890s, and his surname has witnessed a comeback in recent years, as the family's brew has been revived.

Another elaborate mansion from the gilded era now houses the **Indonesian Embassy** *(2020 Massachusetts Ave. N.W. 202-775-5306. By guided tour only; advance reservation required).* Still in grand style both inside and out, this former home of the Walsh family, though now difficult to access, is worth seeing. Its original owner, Thomas Walsh, was an Irish immigrant who made his fortune in Colorado gold and decided to build a mansion to gain him entrée to Washington society. The ploy apparently worked, as his daughter, Evalyn, married into the McLean family, who owned *The Washington Post*. She later became one of the bedeviled owners of the Hope Diamond.

A block north, the renowned 4 **Phillips Collection★★** *(21st and Q Sts. N.W. 202-387-2151. Tues.-Sun.; adm. fee)* stands on a quiet side street. Once home to the prosperous Phillips family, the 1897 brick-and-brownstone house became the first museum of modern art in America when it opened in 1921. At that time, Duncan Phillips, art collector and heir to steel fortunes, opened two rooms of the house as a public gallery. The collection grew steadily, taking over more and more space. Today the entire original building, as well as contemporary additions, stands as testament to Duncan and Marjorie Phillips's discriminating taste. Superb modern masterpieces hang alongside the works of Old Masters like El Greco, though the bulk of the collection concentrates on 19th- and 20th-century art. The intimate galleries display works by Monet, Degas, Cézanne, van Gogh, and Matisse, as well as Renoir, whose Impressionist masterpiece "Luncheon of the Boating Party" (1881) has become the museum's signature piece. One small room is devoted to the whimsical paintings of Swiss visionary Paul Klee, while another gallery surrounds the viewer with the canvases of abstract expressionist Mark Rothko. On Thursday nights, "artful evenings" offer music, lectures, and video presentations.

Politics as Usual

Colorful characters of one sort or the other have long dominated the Washington political scape. One man that typified the best and worst in capital shenanigans was Alexander "Boss" Shepherd, who rose to power during the Grant Administration. Congress had just granted the city independent territorial status, and the high-rolling Shepherd, as overseer of public works, set about improving the city—filling in the unsanitary canal that ran through the heart of town, altering street levels, planting trees, and developing the outlying area around current-day Dupont Circle. While Shepherd's schemes were edifying, they also bankrupted the city, and hence the reputation of the "Boss." In 1874 Congress revoked territorial status and placed the capital city firmly back under congressional control.

Dupont Circle at night

Larz and Isabel Anderson lived nearby on Massachusetts Avenue, in the extravagant, 50-room stone **Anderson House★** *(2118 Massachusetts Ave. N.W. 202-785-2040. Tues.-Sat.)*, built in 1902-05 and donated at Larz's death to the Society of the Cincinnati. A well-traveled diplomat, Ambassador Anderson was a member of the tradition-steeped society that fills its ranks only with eldest-son descendants of Revolutionary War officers. The society's roots go back to 1783, when a group of General Washington's officers looked to the example of sixth-century Roman hero, Lucius Quinctius Cincinnatus, who, according to legend, returned to simple farming life after serving the Roman Republic in a time of civil strife. The lavish national headquarters displays an impressive collection of Revolutionary artifacts; perhaps more breathtaking, however, are the friezes, Renaissance choir stalls, Belgian tapestries, and Hepplewhite and Asian antiques that fill the salons and corridors, all remnants of the Anderson's glorious life here.

Yet another mansion turned exclusive institution stands across the street. The **Cosmos Club** *(2121 Massachusetts Ave. N.W. Private)* occupies a 1901 residence designed to resemble the Petit Trianon at Versailles. Membership is limited to men and women who have contributed to literature, science, or the arts, many of whom have been recipients of Nobel and Pulitzer Prizes.

As Massachusetts Avenue swings around Sheridan

Circle and continues northwest, the embassy presence begins to predominate, with foreign agencies and consulates from around the globe lining the streets. On S Street, two quiet museums interrupt the international milieu. The stately brick 5 **Woodrow Wilson House** *(2340 S St. N.W. 202-387-4062. Tues.-Sun.; adm. fee),* where the 28th President resided after eight trying years in the White House, still fits the description his second wife, Edith Galt Wilson, gave it: "an unpretentious, comfortable, dignified house, fitted to the needs of a gentleman's home." Its gracious, airy rooms contain original Wilson furnishings and offer an intimate glimpse into the private life of this prominent couple. A scholar by nature, Wilson had been president of Princeton University before entering politics. Under his leadership, America entered the First World War, "to make," Wilson proclaimed, "the world safe for democracy." Though he spearheaded the movement for a League of Nations after the war, Congress refused to join the organization, the antecedent to the United Nations. The Norwegian Nobel committee, however, honored Wilson's efforts with the 1919 Nobel Peace Prize. With its proceeds and donations from friends, Wilson and his wife purchased the house on S Street N.W. Having already suffered a serious stroke during his second term, Wilson survived only a few years after leaving office. He died here in 1924, and his body lay in state in the drawing room.

Armor at the Heurich Mansion

The two town houses next door have become the **Textile Museum** *(2320 S St. N.W. 202-667-0441. Donation),* whose extensive collection encompasses the handmade textiles and rugs of Asia, Africa, and South America, with items that date from 3000 B.C. to the present.

The international presence on Massachusetts Avenue culminates in the unmistakable minaret of the white limestone **Islamic Center** *(2551 Massachusetts Ave. N.W. 202-332-8343. Closed Fri. Attire must cover arms, legs, and, for women, heads; shoes must be removed).* The devout gather within the center's mosque five times a day for prayer services. An elaborate blue-tiled colonnade ringing the mosque is decorated with swirling ornamental calligraphy and floral motifs. Positioned at an angle to the street, the mosque faces Mecca, as ordained by Islamic scripture.

Crossing a bridge above Rock Creek Park, you soon see the sweeping green grounds of the 6 **United States Naval Observatory** *(Massachusetts Ave. and Observatory Cir. 202-762-1438. By guided tour only Mon. 8:30-10:00 p.m.).* Established in 1830, the observatory ranked as one of the country's first agencies dedicated solely to scientific research. On its 26-inch telescope, astronomer Asaph Hall discovered the two moons of Mars in 1877. The observatory moved to its present location in 1893, into buildings designed by Richard Morris Hunt. In 1974 the rambling white Victorian that had served as the superintendent's house became the official residence of the Vice President. Besides being a serious astrometry facility devoted to determining the positions of celestial bodies, the observatory is guardian of the Master Clock for the United States. Actually several banks of atomic clocks, they keep the official, to-the-nanosecond time. These and other devices are well explained on the tours.

As Massachusetts Avenue climbs into a more residential area, the overwhelming presence of 7 **Washington National Cathedral**★★ *(Massachusetts and Wisconsin Aves. N.W. 202-364-6616)* looms into view. Crowning Mount St. Albans, this immense Gothic vision is the second largest cathedral in the country and the sixth largest in the world.

Luxembourg Embassy on Embassy Row, along Massachusetts Avenue

Designed in the style of 14th-century Gothic cathedrals, its limestone imminence evokes the spirit with flying buttresses, stained glass, and gargoyles. Its exalted Gloria in Excelsis Tower reaches 300 feet into the sky, defining the horizon in this part of the city, and the 53-bell carillon inside chimes out across the landscape.

Like a true medieval work, this Episcopal Cathedral of Saints Peter and Paul, as it is officially designated, took decades to complete. President Theodore Roosevelt laid the cornerstone in 1907 and President George Bush was on hand when the final stone was set in place in 1990. Though the Episcopal Cathedral Foundation built it, from its inception this was intended as a place of worship and inspiration to all denominations and nationalities.

Thousands of stonemasons, stained-glass artists, and sculptors have dedicated their efforts to the cathedral. A 26-foot-high rose window by artist Rowan LeCompte sheds light throughout the interior. Frederick Hart sculptured the swirling vision of creation that ornaments the tympanum above the central portal, and a multitude of gargoyles peer from the facade. The interior dazzles with even more detail than the exterior. Beneath the vaulted ceiling, soaring a hundred feet, the cavernous nave stretches 565 feet from the narthex, which is inlaid with state seals. Behind the high Jerusalem altar at the far end of the nave, a reredos depicts Christ attended by saints and prophets. Classic Gothic clerestories let in natural light, and state flags fly from the walls.

Washington National Cathedral

Flanking the nave, side aisles lead past small chapels and bays rich in patriotic and religious imagery. The whole sweep of American history is depicted, from George Washington to Woodrow Wilson (who is buried here) to the age of astronauts (a moon rock is embedded in the Space Window). Downstairs in the crypt, intimate chapels glow with candlelight. A seventh-floor observation gallery affords a panoramic view of the region and a close-up glance at the flying buttresses. Outside, 57 acres of quiet gardens and woodlands envelope the cathedral. Three prestigious private schools, a seminary, a greenhouse, and an herb shop are situated on the grounds.

Follow the drive looping behind the cathedral, turn right onto Woodley Road, and right again at 34th Street. After a few blocks turn left onto Cathedral Avenue as it winds through lovely old neighborhoods on its way to Connecticut Avenue, where you turn left.

The Smithsonian Institution's 8 **National Zoological Park★** *(3001 Connecticut Ave. N.W. 202-673-4800)* sprawls across 163 rolling acres, beautifully laid out long ago by landscape architect Frederick Law Olmsted. Since his time, however, the zoo has changed dramatically, and it now calls itself a "biopark," meaning it "focuses on the natural interdependence of life on Earth and integrates elements of the natural sciences, human cultures, and the arts." That may sound like technobabble, but the zoo actually seems to achieve its goal. More than 5,500 animals live in its 18 different exhibit areas, which range from fine old architectural specimens like the whimsically decorated Reptile House (1931) to state-of-the-art wonders like Amazonia, where the rich humidity and the flora and fauna of a tropical rain forest are convincingly re-created. Among the old favorites—elephants, gorillas, seals; lions and tigers and bears—there are also a few rarities. The zoo's most famous residents were Ling-Ling and her consort, Hsing-Hsing, giant pandas presented to the American people by the People's Republic of China. Until Ling-Ling's death in 1992, Washington followed this pair almost as closely as it follows the White House, hoping that the couple would produce offspring. Though Ling-Ling conceived several times, her babies did not survive. Visitors still flock to see Hsing-Hsing.

From the zoo, continue up Connecticut Avenue to Tilden Street and turn right, following Tilden several blocks to Linnean Avenue, where a left turn will soon bring you in sight of the famous walled estate of Post Cereal heiress and Washington hostess, Marjorie Merriweather Post. Her final home, 9 **Hillwood★** *(4155 Linnean Ave. 202-686-5807. Tues.-Sat., closed Feb. Reservations required well in advance; adm. fee),* remains a monument to her extravagant lifestyle, as well as to the opulence of the Russian royal family. Though the brick mansion she built here is unremarkable, it houses the largest collection of Russian decorative arts outside Russia. Marjorie Post intensified her collecting while living in the Soviet Union in the 1930s with her third husband, then the ambassador. The Soviet government had recently begun selling off the bibelots it had seized from the old nobility, and Marjorie took full advantage. Today, Hillwood shimmers with crystal chandeliers, diamond crowns, jewel-encrusted icons, boxes, and Easter eggs created by the famous designer Fabergé for the royal family. One small room is lined with dinner porcelain commissioned by the tsars and tsarinas. Even the plates on which Catherine the Great dined are on display.

At the Smithsonian Institution's National Zoo

Sharing Catherine's free spirit, Mrs. Post was married four times and maintained a vigorous social schedule, entertaining extravagantly. The dining room table, inlaid with Florentine marble, seats 30 guests, and behind the house a rustic, Adirondack-style cottage houses the Native American rugs, basketry, and pottery that decorated Mrs. Post's Adirondack country estate. Nearby, a small log *dacha* is filled with more Russian art. The most serene spot on the estate is the Japanese garden.

Return to Tilden Street and continue downhill to the 1820s **Pierce Mill** *(Intersection of Tilden St. and Beach Dr. 202-426-6908. Wed.-Sun.)*, recalling the days when a line of gristmills stood at intervals along Rock Creek. Inside, National Park Service rangers explain how such mills worked, and tell of the Quaker family who established the mill as part of an extensive agricultural operation that took in thousands of acres. Their old stone carriage house is now the **Rock Creek Gallery,** displaying works by local artists. Mill and barn are now surrounded by **Rock Creek Park,** a 1,750-acre natural area that snakes through Northwest, following the lovely little valley cut by Rock Creek. Bicyclists, horseback riders, birders, and picnickers flock here to enjoy the sylvan setting.

At **Beach Drive** *(One-way during rush hours, partially closed to vehicles on weekends),* the park's main thoroughfare, turn right and wind through the rock-riven valley of the creek, passing the rear entrance of the zoo along the way. Beach Drive dead-ends at the Rock Creek and Potomac Parkway, where you bear left. In about a mile, the parkway passes under two successive stone bridges. After the latter take an immediate, sharp right up the ramp, then left onto P Street, and you'll find yourself at the eastern edge of ⑩ **Georgetown★.** Here, narrow streets squeeze past stylish Victorian and federal row houses occupied by some of the country's most influential citizens. Predating Washington itself, this elegant enclave at the confluence of Rock Creek and the Potomac River sprang to life in the mid-1700s as a colonial port and did not become part of the capital until 1871. Though it languished during the early 1900s, it regained its footing in mid-century when prominent Washingtonians like John and Jacqueline Kennedy began purchasing and restoring the neighborhood's gracious old homes. Today, Georgetown's side streets are bastions of quiet taste, while its two intersecting commercial streets—Wisconsin Avenue and M Street—teem with activity. By day, shoppers browse the shops; by night, the area's restaurants and clubs attract the refined and the rambunctious.

Breakfast room, Hillwood

The epitome of Georgetown taste lies in the hushed, walled enclave of ⑪ **Dumbarton Oaks★** *(32nd St. N.W. between R and S Sts. 202-339-6401. Tues.-Sun.; donation).* The dignified brick house at its core dates from 1800. In 1920 the estate was purchased by diplomat Robert Bliss and his wife, Mildred. They transformed it into an elegant showcase, and eventually gave it to Harvard University to operate as a museum and research institution. The Dumbarton Oaks Conference held here in 1944 eventually led to the formation of the United Nations. Today, the Bliss's

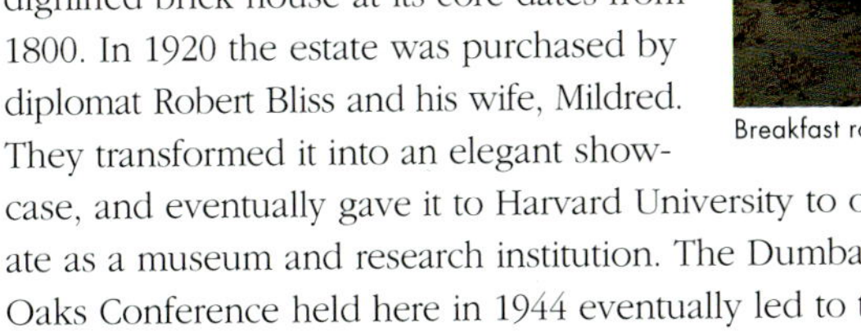

extensive collection of Byzantine coins, silver, and icons is displayed around a Mediterranean-style interior courtyard. The music room, decorated in the style of a French château, is hung with European tapestries, and a modern wing by architect Philip Johnson features eight circular, glass-enclosed pavilions. This rarefied setting was designed specifically to show off the Bliss's superb collection of pre-Columbian figurines, gold, masks, and tapestries.

The famous **Dumbarton Oaks Gardens** *(Fee)* cascade down a hillside in a series of terraces celebrating different floral and cultural motifs. Just down R Street, **Oak Hill Cemetery** *(202-337-2835. Mon.-Fri.)* ranges across the hillsides above Rock Creek. The small, brick Gothic Revival chapel near the entrance is the work of James Renwick, architect of the Renwick Gallery building and the Smithsonian Castle.

Another fine Georgetown house, **Tudor Place** *(31st and Q Sts. N.W. 202-965-0400. Tues.-Sat.; donation)* stands on its own knoll nearby. The structure was built at the beginning of the 19th century by Martha Custis Peter, granddaughter of Martha Washington, and occupied by their descendants until 1983. The decor of the house spans these six generations and chronicles the social history and changing tastes of the nation's capital. The federal house, designed by U.S. Capitol architect Dr. William Thornton, is protected from the encroachments of modern day by its own five acres of landscaped lawn and gardens.

Federal row houses in Georgetown

At the southern edge of Georgetown, just above the Potomac River, runs the 12 **Chesapeake and Ohio (C&O) Canal** *(301-299-3613)*, now a national historical park. From Rock Creek, it starts its 184.5-mile journey north to Cumberland, Maryland. Built as an early 19th-century shipping route for goods and travelers moving back and forth from the heartland to the coast, the canal, with its 74 lift locks, has become a major recreation corridor. The old towpath now bustles with bikers and hikers who seek out its quiet, wooded environs next to the Potomac. Though some areas of the pathway were wrecked by recent flooding, governmental and private organizations are working to repair the damage. In Georgetown charming little row houses face the canal, giving the area a European feel. At lift lock number three, a bust of U.S. Supreme Court

Georgetown's Washington Harbor, with the John F. Kennedy Center for the Performing Arts in the background

Justice William O. Douglas commemorates his efforts to have the canal preserved as a recreational greenway.

The **Old Stone House** *(3051 M St. N.W. 202-426-6851. Donation)* has watched over the bustle on M Street since 1765. The Park Service has outfitted the modest bluestone house as it would have looked when woodworker and joiner Christopher Layman built it.

Of Georgetown's many picturesque blocks, a particularly worthwhile stroll leads down the 3200-3300 blocks of N Street. The first block here boasts a perfect line of federal row houses known as **Smith's Row,** still preserving their original circa 1815 character. The second block, **Cox's Row,** features five more elaborate houses from the 1790s. The one at 3307 N Street was purchased by Senator John F. Kennedy and his wife, Jacqueline, in 1957. This area has a distinctly collegiate feel to it, as it borders 13 **Georgetown University,** established in 1789 as the first Catholic institution of higher learning in the country. Now renowned for its international affairs programs, the university boasts a lovely gray stone quadrangle, whose spired halls punctuate the skyline in this part of the city.

To return to the National Geographic, follow P Street east to Dupont Circle. At the far side of the circle, veer right onto Massachusetts Avenue, and turn right several blocks down onto 17th Street to reach your starting point.

Along the Potomac★★

● 45 miles ● 2 days ● Year-round

This drive along the shores of the Potomac River begins at the military heart of the nation—the huge, nondescript fortress known worldwide as the **1 Pentagon★** *(Follow signs for Pentagon City Mall off I-395. 703-695-1776. Mon.-Fri. Tours require photo ID. Park at Pentagon City Mall).* The largest single-structure federal office building in the world, its 6.6 million square feet radiate out in five concentric pentagons surrounding a 5-acre open-air courtyard, known by the grisly nickname "ground zero." Constructed in a flurry of patriotic zeal during World World II, the Pentagon was completed in just 16 months, in January 1943. Obviously a high security place, tours take in only public hallways and ceremonial spaces, but its vast Byzantine quality comes through clearly.

From the Pentagon, take Va. 27 north to the traffic circle at the foot of Memorial Bridge. Veer counterclockwise three-quarters of the way around to Memorial Drive and follow signs for **Arlington National Cemetery★★** *(703-607-8052).* Encompassing 612 rolling acres above the Potomac, the shaded grounds, with their rows of simple white headstones, are hauntingly beautiful in any season. In addition to thousands of veterans, the grounds hold the tombs of President John F. Kennedy, remembered by an eternal flame, and his brother Robert. A ceremonial changing of the guard takes place hourly at the Tomb of the Unknowns, where unidentified bodies of soldiers from World Wars I and II and the Korean and Vietnam Wars are buried.

The cemetery is actually situated on the former grounds of **Arlington House** *(703-557-0613),* the Greek Revival home of Robert E. and Mary Lee. Built between 1802 and 1817 by George Washington Parke Custis, Mary's father and the step-grandson of George Washington, the house graces a bluff overlooking the Potomac and the capital. When the Civil War broke out, Union forces quickly moved to

Arlington National Cemetery

secure this high ground, and, in an act of vengeance, the Army's quartermaster general suggested the grounds be used as a Federal cemetery. The Lees never returned to Arlington House, though Robert professed that his "affections and attachments" were "more strongly placed" there "than at any other place in the world." The house retains a few Lee furnishings and Victorian decor of the Lee era.

Just beyond the house's columned veranda, with its long view out to Washington, a marble plaque marks the tomb of Pierre L'Enfant, the 18th-century French architect who designed the federal city. L'Enfant died embittered and in debt, and not until 1909 were his remains reinterred here, giving him a view of the city he envisioned.

From the cemetery, retrace your route back to the Pentagon and follow signs for I-395 south and then I-95 south. After about 8 miles, take the Lorton exit and follow signs along US 1 to 2 **Gunston Hall**★ *(Gunston Rd., Mason Neck.*

703-550-9220. Adm. fee). The former home of colonial statesman George Mason, the mansion is an exemplary relic of Georgian architecture, set at the end of a long allée of magnolias. The estate is renowned for its towering and extensive boxwood gardens and for the elegant woodwork that graces the plantation house interior. William Buckland, who came from England under an indenture, designed the woodwork for Mason and went on to establish a wide reputation among the colonial gentry as a master craftsman.

Mason himself also enjoyed a high reputation, described by his colleague Thomas Jefferson as "a man of the first order of wisdom." Though he disliked the fray of open politics, Mason exerted profound, behind-the-scenes influence on colonial and early federal government. His wording in the Virginia Declaration of Rights (June 1776), "That all men are by nature equally free and independent and have certain inherent rights..." was closely echoed one month later in the Declaration of Independence. Though Mason owned slaves, he saw problems concerning slavery's compatibility with the designs of democracy and refused, among other reasons, to sign the Constitution because it did not ban the importation of slaves. (He also thought it made the federal government too strong.)

Return to US 1 and follow it north roughly 5 miles to **Woodlawn Plantation**★ *(9000 Richmond Hwy. 703-780-4000. Daily March-Dec., weekends Jan.-Feb.; adm. fee).* The charming brick Georgian, built at the turn of the 19th century, embodies the sophistication and hopes of the new nation. It was the home of Nelly and Lawrence Lewis, both close relatives of George Washington, who bequeathed the land to them. Nelly, granddaughter of Martha Washington, had been raised at Mount Vernon, where, as a young woman, she met Washington's nephew, Lawrence Lewis.

The design of their house is attributed to Capitol architect Dr. William Thornton. Amid its well-appointed surroundings, the Custises held legendary soirees and entertained the cream of early American society, including war hero Lafayette. The family's fine possessions, including a number of pieces from Mount Vernon, again ornament the interior of this gracious house, though it now stands perilously close to the ungainly hubbub of US 1.

The National Trust for Historic Preservation, which owns Woodlawn, has transplanted another historic piece of architecture to the grounds. The modest, low-slung

Virginia's Historic Garden Week

For more than 60 years now, the Old Dominion has been celebrating its wealth of historic—and more contemporary—houses during the last full week of April. Then, when the dogwoods and azaleas are at their showiest, hundreds of private residences otherwise closed to the public throw open their doors. The schedule rotates geographically day by day, with homes in a specific area open only for one or two days of the week. Museums, gardens, and other public attractions join the festivities. *(Historic Garden Club of Virginia 804-644-7776. Adm. tickets sold by locality)*

Gunston Hall

Pope-Leighey House was designed by Frank Lloyd Wright in 1939 as an example of his Usonian architecture—small, affordable homes for the middle class. The simple horizontal lines of the house are classic Wright, as are the built-in furnishings. The house was again restored in 1996, and a provocative tour explains the architectural elements Wright used in his design.

From Woodlawn, follow Va. 235 east 3 miles passing along the way, on a millrace off Dogue Creek, a towering stone **gristmill** that was once part of George Washington's properties. Soon after, the drive draws up in front of 3 **Mount Vernon**★★ *(South end of George Washington Mem. Pkwy. and Va. 235. 703-780-2000. Adm. fee).* George Washington's plantation holds a unique place in the national psyche, and about a million visitors a year throng here to pay homage at his large estate on the bluffs above the Potomac. The landmark mansion, with its red roof, cupola, and wide veranda facing the river, began as a small farmhouse built by Washington's father in the 1730s. George actually acquired the land through his half brother and benefactor, Lawrence, and spent years expanding and decorating the manor. Though war and politics kept him away from his beloved home for much of his life, Washington apparently was happiest here. He considered farming "the most delectable occupation" and was exceedingly good at it. His properties in the area encompassed some 8,000 acres, divided into five farms. Washington died here on December 14, 1799, saying, "I die hard but I am not afraid to go." He was 67.

Though Washington characterized his life here as a simple, "republican style of living," the decor at Mount

Rear veranda overlooking the Potomac River, Mount Vernon

Vernon reflects the fashions of his time, with brightly painted rooms and ornate trim. A great deal of the furniture in the house today was chosen by him. Much as he hoped to return to a quiet life here, he and Martha were hounded by admiring guests. "Scarcely any strangers who are going from north to south, or from south to north, do not spend a day or two...," Washington wrote.

Washington's busy farm life is recalled in more than a dozen standing outbuildings scattered across the estate—curing, spinning, laundry, dairy houses, and more. A small museum displays more family memorabilia and a bust of the general by Jean-Antoine Houdon. George and Martha lie in a brick vault, surrounded by other family members, off the lawn sweeping from the mansion's piazza to the river.

From Mount Vernon, the drive turns north, following lovely **George Washington Memorial Parkway** along the Potomac River and affording fine views out across its tidal flats. A paved hiking and biking path travels between the parkway and Potomac. At **Dyke Marsh Wildlife Preserve** near Belle Haven, a trail winds into a marsh full of shorebirds and migratory flocks. About 8 miles from Mount Vernon, the parkway becomes Washington Street as it enters **4 Old Town Alexandria★★.** Just down the Potomac from Washington's cosmopolitan milieu, this enclave maintains a style far different from the sometimes maddening machinations of the capital. Priding themselves on their more mannerly Southern ways, the well-heeled townsfolk have restored to tony perfection the colonial and federal houses that line the shaded side streets here. Parks, cruise ships, and festive piers edge the Potomac waterfront, and the restaurants, cafés, and live-music bars along King Street make for probably the liveliest night scene in the state.

Chartered in the mid-1700s, the town was laid out in grid fashion and quickly became a robust seaport, with a decidedly Scots tenor. As the colonial hub of the region, it boasted a cadre of notables, including Lord Fairfax and George Washington. Today, the town celebrates its colonial roots at various sites. The best way to tour the 30-block historic core is on foot. Walking tour maps and other information are available at **Ramsay House Visitor Center** *(King and N. Fairfax Sts. 703-838-4200),* a small clapboard whose north end now ranks as the city's oldest structure (1724), though it was moved here from an outlying area.

For 250 years the focus of King Street has been **Market Square** *(Between N. Fairfax and N. Royal Sts.),* now backed by the stolid brick facade of the 1873 Victorian city hall. Fountains gush here in summer, and on weekends year-round the square becomes a true marketplace. At first light every Saturday morning, produce and flower vendors arrive to sell their wares. In summer, craft fairs, free concerts, and ethnic festivals often take place here.

Shop signs, Old Town Alexandria

Nearby is another vintage site, the **Stabler-Leadbeater Apothecary Museum** *(105-107 S. Fairfax St. 703-836-3713. Adm. fee).* The historic shop-museum occupies two town houses. The older Georgian (1775), on the left, housed the original shop run by Quaker entrepreneur and apothecary, Edward Stabler, at the turn of the 18th century. Edward's heirs continued to do business here until the shop closed its doors in 1933. Original medical jars and herbal cures again fill its shelves, and the Windsor chair where client Robert E. Lee occasionally sat stands at the back. The museum's archival collection holds a wealth of information on

Alexandria's history and the development of pharmaceuticals over almost two centuries.

The most imposing dwelling in town, **Carlyle House**★ *(121 N. Fairfax St. 703-549-2997. Closed Mon.; adm. fee)* stands in Georgian splendor, surrounded by grounds and gardens. Scottish entrepreneur John Carlyle built the stone manor house in the 1750s, when his lands actually fronted the Potomac. (Landfill has since added streets between house and waterfront.) In April 1755, British Gen. Edward Braddock held a Governors' Council here, in which he elicited financial support from five royal governors and their districts for the British war against the French and Indians. Knowing their constituencies would balk, the governors refused—an early sign that the British were losing control over the hearts and minds of the colonists. Now outfitted in the neat and plain style of mid-18th-century America, the house does a good job recreating life in the colonial port.

The nearby **Torpedo Factory**★ *(105 N. Union St.)* has become one of the city's most compelling attractions. Its battleship-gray exterior recalls that this was indeed a torpedo factory during World War II. But in the last few decades, it has been reborn as a highly successful arts-and-crafts center. From their studios here, painters, potters, weavers, and jewelers sell finely made products. Also located on site is a small museum called **Alexandria Archaeology** *(703-838-4399. Tues.-Sun.)*, containing a lab and artifacts recovered from city digs.

Torpedo Factory artisan center, Alexandria

Perhaps the quaintest block in Old Town lies at the lower end of Prince Street *(bet. S. Union and Lee Sts.)*, where small, aged town houses are wedged. The cobblestones that pave what is known as **Captain's Row** came across the Atlantic as ballast in the holds of ships. The block above is called **Gentry Row** for the handsome 18th-century town houses that line it.

Many of the gentry attended services at the **Old Presbyterian Meeting House** *(321 S. Fairfax St. 703-549-6670),* whose upright character has graced the town's south end since 1775. The good Scotsman, John Carlyle, oversaw its building, and he, along with other prominent Alexandrians, are interred in the churchyard. Public funeral services for George Washington were held here in 1799, and the church bell tolled four days in mourning. The original church was almost entirely destroyed by lightning in 1835, but it was quickly rebuilt along its simple lines.

Candlelit window, Gadsby's Tavern Museum, Alexandria

Gadsby's Tavern Museum★ *(134 N. Royal St. 703-838-4242. Tues.-Sun.; adm. fee)* witnessed a lot of the nation's early history. The inn, actually two separate town houses, played host to figures like Jefferson, Adams, and others in the early 19th century. At that time Alexandria was part of the newly created federal city, now called Washington, D.C. But since the capital's core was then swampland, the infant country's luminaries chose to hostel themselves amid the relative comforts of well-established Alexandria. Harkening back to that early heyday, the tavern now recreates the period in its private dining rooms, vast ballroom, and small bedchambers, where guests enjoyed varying degrees of comfort.

At **Christ Church** *(Cameron and N. Washington Sts. 703-549-1450)* high brick walls enclose a peaceful setting. The church raises its peppermill steeple above the churchyard trees and weathered gravestones. Completed in 1773 by the ubiquitous John Carlyle, the church is proud of its connections to Washington and Lee, marking with plaques the pews in which each worshiped. On President's Day, the sitting Chief Executive often comes to worship in Washington's pew.

Lee spent much of his boyhood just up the street at the intersection of North Washington and Oronoco Streets, a spot so well populated by his relatives that it became known as Lee Corner. In the 1780s, Lee's father, Light Horse Harry, sold the piece of property on the southeast corner to a relative, Philip Fendall, who built the current substantial clapboard now known as the **Lee-Fendall House** *(614 Oronoco St. 703-548-1789. Tues.-Sun., call for hours; adm. fee).* Lees occupied the house for more than a hundred years, until the mid-20th century when the house became home of famous labor leader, John L. Lewis. The furnishings now reflect the Lees' life here in the mid-19th century, with a number of their family pieces.

The **Boyhood Home of Robert E. Lee** *(607 Oronoco St. 703-548-8454. Feb.–mid-Dec.; adm. fee)* stands across the street. The federal town house (1795), though ample, is a far cry from his manorial birthplace, Stratford Hall. Lee spent a rather frugal childhood here, after his father lost the family fortune in land speculation. When Robert was six, Light Horse Harry sailed to Barbados, presumably to recover his health. Five years later, he died on Cumberland Island, Georgia, and Robert became his invalid mother's strong arm. Inside the house hang five contemporary portraits depicting Lee over time, from handsome West Point graduate to aging general.

Along the Virginia side of the Potomac River

Though Alexandria was occupied by the Union for most of the Civil War, the town had deep Southern sympathies, and a statue of a Confederate soldier overlooks the town's Greek Revival **Lyceum, Alexandria's History Museum** *(201 S. Washington St. 703-838-4994. Donation).* Constructed as a "cultural center" in the 1830s, it still serves that function with galleries tracing the city's history. Nearby the **Friendship Firehouse Museum** *(107 S. Alfred St. 703-838-3891. Fri.-Sun.)* dates from 1855 and displays trucks and implements of 19th-century fire fighting.

Backtrack to the George Washington Memorial Parkway and continue north, watching the Washington skyline pressed into the horizon as you travel the roughly 5 miles to 5 **Theodore Roosevelt Island** *(Parking lot just off Pkwy. bet. Roosevelt and Key Bridges; take footbridge to island).* Floating in the Potomac across from the capital's John F. Kennedy Center for the Performing Arts, this is a fine natural spot, with paths looping through woodlands, and a clearing where a strident Teddy stands with arm upraised—a fitting memorial to the man who fathered the National Park System.

Turn right as you leave the island's parking lot and take the Spout Run exit. A left-hand turnaround allows you to loop down and back onto the parkway heading south.

Piedmont Loop ★★

● 185 miles ● 2 days ● Spring through fall

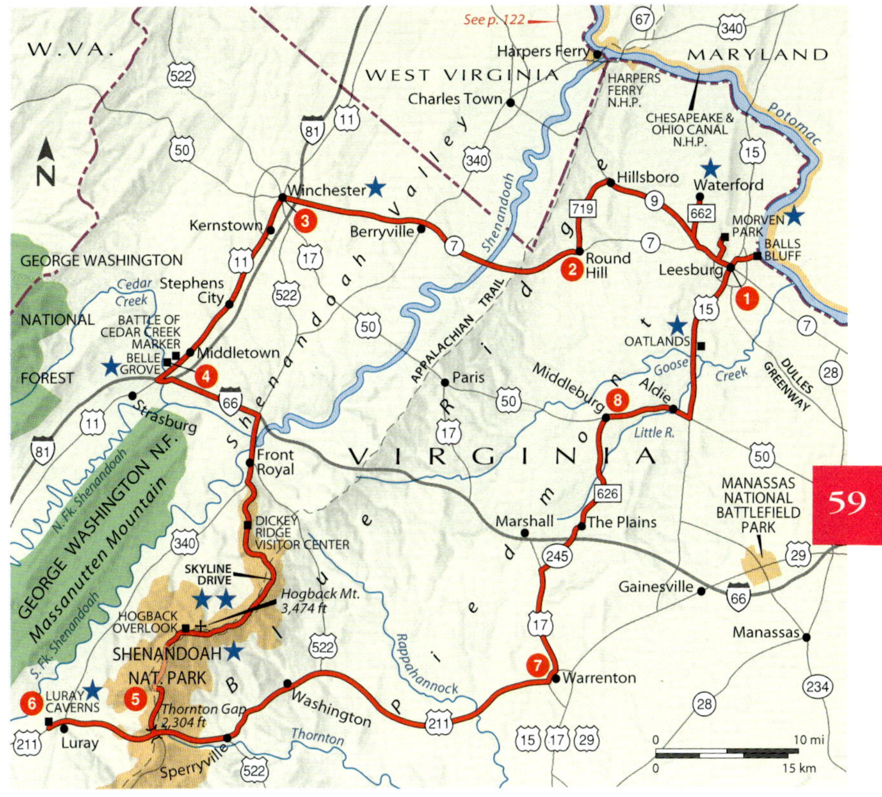

Weaving through classic Virginia Piedmont, the country lanes and byways of this drive dip past soft-spoken small towns, lush farmlands, and perfect green pastures where handsome Thoroughbreds peacefully graze. The drive then enters the north end of the Shenandoah Valley, visiting history-rich Winchester and picking up the trail of the Civil War before swinging up onto the crest of the Blue Ridge along the renowned Skyline Drive. The route cuts briefly west to ever popular Luray Caverns before following the rushing Thornton River into the little crafts center of Sperryville. From here, it moves northwest, back into the Piedmont, through some of the state's finest horse country and past the superb old estate of Oatlands, where the grandeur of the antebellum past remains a thing of the present.

Begin in **1** **Leesburg** *(Visitor Center 703-777-0519 or*

800-752-6118), once hub of the old farming county of Loudoun and now the far edge of Washington's urban sprawl. Still picturesque and low-key, its narrow downtown streets, edged by federal- and Victorian-era buildings, now brim with upscale shops, restaurants, and browsing suburbanites. The city's rich past is well documented at the **Loudoun Museum** *(Loudoun and Wirt Sts. 703-777-7427. Closed Jan.),* where exhibits and a video explain the county's colonial roots, Civil War heritage, and prosperous modern period. Next door, the small log cabin of a mid-18th-century silversmith now holds the museum gift shop. The museum's guided walking tours travel past some 50 historic structures, including the Italianate brick courthouse, guarded by the de rigueur statue of a Confederate soldier.

Loudoun County Courthouse, Leesburg

For a further look at Loudoun's blended past and present, drive out to **Ball's Bluff Regional Park** *(Off US 15 Bypass N, take Battlefield Pkwy. to Ball's Bluff Rd.).* This small but important Civil War site lies in the woods at the eastern edge of Leesburg's suburban sprawl. In the eerie quiet, a three-quarter-mile trail leads past interpretive signs explaining the battle fought here in October 1861, when invading Union troops were sent scurrying back across the Potomac. Scattered headstones mark the small national cemetery.

Morven Park★ *(Morven Park Dr. and Old Waterford Rd. 703-777-2414. Closed Mon. April-Oct., open weekends in Nov.; adm. fee)* basks in its own glow. The shimmering white, 19th-century mansion, with its columned neoclassical veranda, hovers above a tumbling green where the appearance of horsemen in riding pinks seems imminent. Home to Maryland governor Thomas Swann in the 19th century, it is better known for its later tenant, Virginia governor Westmoreland Davis, who lived here early in this century. Its rich Flemish tapestries and formal European furnishings are redolent of the old hunt country élan. The estate's 1,200 acres also include a boxwood garden, the **Museum of Hounds and Hunting,** and a carriage collection.

Leaving Leesburg, follow Va. 7 west to Va. 9 north, turning off onto bucolic Rte. 662. Moseying past picturesque dairy farms and country fields for a couple of miles, the road ambles into **Waterford★★,** perhaps the most charming village in the state. Established as a Quaker milling center 250 years ago and now a national historic landmark district, Waterford rises and falls over rolling hills, the two-story verandas of its simple colonial and substantial federal houses overlooking streets lost in time. Virtually every house in town has a noteworthy past, and the townsfolk, ardent preservationists, allow almost nothing commercial to sully the mood—except for the annual **Waterford Homes Tour & Crafts Exhibit** *(540-882-3085. First Fri.-Sun. in Oct.),* which draws artisans and shoppers from throughout the mid-Atlantic.

Returning to Va. 9 north, the drive continues 7 miles into **Hillsboro,** a lovely wayside that in two blocks flaunts several old stone houses from the last century. At the north end of town, turn left onto Rte. 719, a narrow black ribbon dividing broad expanses of farm fields backed by the distant Blue Ridge mountains. Where the road bends sharply left, look for the ruined stone skeleton of an old cider mill. After about 7 miles Rte. 719 leads to the small town of 2 **Round Hill.** Turn right onto Va. 7, a main route west. Several miles east of the pleasant farming hub of Berryville, the route crests a ridge, and the Shenandoah Valley suddenly unfolds below.

Countryside near Winchester

About a half dozen miles beyond Berryville sits the town of 3 **Winchester★** *(Visitor Center 540-662-4135 or 800-662-1360),* the only real city in this far northwestern corner of the state and the northern gateway to both the

Shenandoah and the South. Because of its strategic location, the site was fought over many times during the Civil War. In the four years of that conflict, the flag flying above the town changed 72 times. An old-style Southern charm now permeates the town, making it a perfect setting for the area's annual Shenandoah Apple Blossom Festival, held the first weekend in May. Winchester's history is clustered in a few pleasantly walkable blocks of downtown, where many old buildings wear a ghostly white facade of local limestone; a two-block pedestrian mall holds an eclectic mix of establishments, from New Age shops to old-time variety stores.

To orient yourself, stop for walking tour maps at the **Kurtz Cultural Center** *(2 N. Cameron St. 540-722-6367),* housed in a Victorianized 1836 warehouse. Besides special traveling exhibits, usually on historical themes, the center details the many battles that took place in the Shenandoah during the Civil War. A showcase here also honors local legend Patsy Cline, a Winchester girl who meteorically rose to country music stardom before her life ended in a tragic plane crash. Explorer Robert E. Byrd and authors Willa Cather and Russell Baker were also born in these parts.

Victorian house along Fairmont Street, Winchester

Two blocks west stands a simple stone-and-wood cabin, now immortalized as **George Washington's Office Museum** *(Braddock and Cork Sts. 540-662-4412. April-Oct.; adm. fee).* The little building was occupied by the young lieutenant colonel in the mid-1700s, while he supervised the building of Fort Loudoun. Now it holds colonial surveying tools, militia memorabilia, and other artifacts relating to the town's early years.

A different era is commemorated in the ample brick Gothic Revival house that served as **Stonewall Jackson's Headquarters** *(415 N. Braddock St. 540-667-3242. April-Oct.; adm. fee).* Jackson had not yet achieved hero status when he quartered here during the winter of 1861-62—the following spring he undertook the brilliant Valley Campaign through the Shenandoah that would earn him a place in the annals of military history. In what were perhaps his most peaceful days of the war, Jackson passed his Winchester winter in the company of his second wife, Mary Anne. Stonewall admirers will be interested in such personal items as Jackson's camp table and prayer book, now on display in the comfortable old house. In an odd footnote to the story, Jackson's host in the house was Lt. Col. Lewis Moore, whose great-granddaughter, actress Mary Tyler Moore, donated the ornate gilded wallpaper now hanging there.

Costumed boy at Civil War reenactment, Cedar Creek

Jackson was not the only Civil War hero to headquarter in town. Union Gen. Phil Sheridan stayed just a few blocks away in another large Victorian. But the old Southern town sees no reason to celebrate his stay, and the house now holds a shop.

Both Union and Confederate are honored, however, out off Pleasant Valley Road, where rows of simple white gravestones line the **National Cemetery,** and similar rows march across the **Stonewall Cemetery.** Continue south on this road to **Abram's Delight Museum** *(540-662-6519. April-Oct.; adm. fee).* The substantial two-story stone house, built in 1754 and now the town's oldest private home, is thought to have served as Winchester's first Quaker meetinghouse.

Leaving town on US 11 south—the old Valley Pike—the drive heads into the Shenandoah, where one roadside marker after another tells the story of Civil War battles. The marker at **Kernstown,** just off US 11, explains the opening salvo in Jackson's Valley Campaign. After his first battle here in March 1862, Jackson and the 17,000 men of his redoubtable "foot cavalry" spent two months weaving in and out of passes in the mountains, appearing and reappearing to attack and befuddle some 60,000 Union soldiers. But that was the heyday of the Confederate cause. A year later Jackson was dead, and by the autumn of 1864, the Shenandoah was about to fall to Phil Sheridan, the tough, bandy-legged cavalry commander that Grant had sent into the Shenandoah to "make of it a wasteland, so that even

Autumn at Hogback Overlook, Skyline Drive, Shenandoah National Park

crows flying over must carry their own provender."

About 10 miles down the pike, the drive passes a marker for the **Battle of Cedar Creek,** where Sheridan had one of his finest moments. In October of 1864, with his troops encamped here, Sheridan went to Washington to confer with officials, then returned to spend the night in Winchester. In his absence the feisty Confederate commander Jubal Early launched a surprise attack on the Union troops. Hearing of it in Winchester, Sheridan dashed to the field, forcing his routed army into a successful counterattack.

The battlefield today slumbers in a pastoral roll of hills overlooked by the mighty Georgian mansion of 4 **Belle Grove★** *(540-869-2028. Mid-March–Oct.; adm. fee),* where Sheridan headquartered. But the imposing stone manse, with its stolid six chimneys and quoined corners, has a much longer pedigree. Isaac Hite, Jr., built the home in the late 1700s, enlisting his brother-in-law, James Madison, to assist in its design. The perfect classical proportions of the house, now a National Trust property, suggest that Madison, in turn, may have had a little help from his friend, inveterate architect Thomas Jefferson.

From Belle Grove continue south briefly on the old Valley Pike, then head east on I-66, which, despite its interstate status, offers superb scenery. Rounding the northern end of Massanutten Mountain, the highway

angles through stony pastureland where cattle balance on hillsides and hawks survey the countryside from the bleached limbs of oak snags. Exit at **Front Royal** *(Visitor Center 540-635-3185)*, yet another quiet Shenandoah town that clings to its Civil War past. This one is particularly proud of its association with the flamboyant Southern spy Belle Boyd. No wilting lily, Belle once shot a Union soldier she suspected of insulting her mother. The **Belle Boyd Cottage** *(101 Chester St. 540-636-1446. May-Oct. Mon.-Fri. and weekends by appt., Nov.-April by appt.; adm. fee)*, a simple, two-story clapboard, was the home of Boyd's aunt and uncle during the war, and Belle visited here often, using her feminine charms to elicit information from Union troops occupying the town. The cottage now offers a history of the area—and of Belle—during the war. The adjacent Ivy Lodge houses more local history exhibits. The **Warren Rifles Confederate Museum** *(95 Chester St. 540-636-6982. Mid-April–mid-Nov.; adm. fee)* also commemorates local heroes of the war.

From Front Royal, take US 340 a mile south to the entrance of 5 **Shenandoah National Park★** *(540-999-3500. Adm. fee)*. One of the nation's most visited parks, it is ribboned by the 105-mile **Skyline Drive★★,** which weaves and bobs along the northern Blue Ridge. Curving up through dappled hardwood forests, the drive climbs 2 miles to the Shenandoah Valley Overlook, where the age-old valley, once the haunt of Indians and buffalo, yawns peacefully below. Two miles beyond, the **Dickey Ridge Visitor Center** *(April–mid-Nov.)* offers information on hiking trails, including the Maine-to-Georgia

Deer along Skyline Drive

Appalachian Trail, which runs the length of the park.

For the next 100 miles, Skyline Drive follows the crest of the Blue Ridge, the long, low smoke-blue range that defines the eastern edge of the Shenandoah Valley. Designed to complement the landscape, the drive sweeps serenely along the ridgetop, its old stone guardrails growing out of the ground almost like natural features. The Civilian Conservation Corps built the original guardrails and much of the landscape and recreational features along the drive. The road itself, opened in the 1930s when the park was formed, displaced many mountainfolk in the process. Viewpoints along the way look down on the hollows that once held their homesteads. But nature, as much as progress, brought an end to their lifestyle in the 1920s, when the chestnut trees they depended on for food, firewood, and lumber died by blight.

At **Hogback Overlook** you can see the South Fork Shenandoah River curling like a glossy snake past farms and forests. The road continues to wind past several other overlooks to the first exit, at Thornton Gap. Here, leave Skyline Drive by taking US 211 west for 11 miles to the state's premier subterranean attraction, 6 **Luray Caverns**★ *(Va. 211. 540-743-6551. Adm. fee).* Caverns riddle the Virginia ground in this area, and many are operated as commercial ventures. But Luray ranks as the grande dame of them all. Not exactly a spelunking adventure, Luray is laced with paved trails that weave up and around the cave's well-lit, spectacular stalactites, stalagmites, draperies, and flowstone. You can even "hear rocks sing" when the Great Stalactite Organ lets loose its sonorous booms.

From Luray, retrace your steps on US 211, then head east through Thornton Gap. Tumbling down into a small hollow, you pass the craft shops of local quilters, potters, and other artisans that cluster in the little hamlet of **Sperryville.** The landscape opens up now into pastureland edged by the distant frill of forests.

Passing through a brief commercial strip in the town of 7 **Warrenton,** the drive picks up US 17 north for 8 miles, then jags briefly right on Va. 245, which quickly connects with Rte. 626. This stretch encompasses an elegant, bucolic setting, with Thoroughbred horses lounging in roadside fields. Their owners are often scions of American industry and politics, all drawn to the hunt country around 8 **Middleburg** *(Visitor Center 540-687-8888),* about 15 miles

Virginia Wines

Before New York, California, and all those other states, the Old Dominion tried its hand at making wine. The first Jamestown diehards managed to produce a wine of sorts from native grapes. But it wasn't until the 1830s that an American hybrid called the Norton Virginia gave the state a claret that would be admired throughout America and in Europe. It took another century and a half before wine production in Virginia truly burgeoned. Now vineyards flourish throughout the state, though most are located in the mid- to northern Piedmont. *(For information on winery locations, tours, and tastings, call 800-828-4637 and request the "Virginia Wineries—Festival and Tour Guide" pamphlet.)*

down the road. A traveler's crossroads since the 1730s, the town has several wayside taverns worth a stop. If you haven't had your fill of the Civil War, try the **Red Fox Inn** *(2 E. Washington St. 540-478-1808),* a stone building that claims to be the nation's oldest original inn. Its dark rooms were once frequented by John Singleton Mosby, the South's famous Gray Ghost. He and his Partisan Rangers so harassed Union forces venturing into this part of the state that the area became known as Mosby's Confederacy.

From Middleburg, turn east on US 50 and follow the Little River for 7 miles, passing the quaint old mill at Aldie along the way. The drive now turns onto US 15 north back toward Leesburg. Midway there, you'll see the long allée that announces **Oatlands★** *(US 15. 703-777-3174. April-Dec.; adm. fee).* Reflecting more than a century of tastes and styles, the white stone mansion stands with lofty fluted columns raised in welcome. The house's original owner, George Carter, was a great-grandson of colonial land baron, Robert "King" Carter. The Civil War laid a hard hand on Oatlands and for a while it functioned as a kind of boardinghouse. But later owners, the Eustices, restored it to its former grandeur. As impressive as the house are the exuberant restored gardens that plunge down hillside terraces overlooking the surrounding countryside.

Red Fox Inn, Middleburg

Northern Neck★

● 115 miles ● 2 days ● Spring through fall

Virginians call the verdant green bulge of land lying between the Rappahannock and Potomac Rivers the Northern Neck. This drive begins at the upper end of the neck in Fredericksburg, a longtime river and rail center that repeatedly came under fire in the Civil War. From here, the route weaves through the fertile lands of this peninsula, whose fields have spawned such heroes as George Washington and Robert E. Lee. Washington spent his boyhood here on the shores of the Potomac, and two sites now commemorate his youth. Not far from Washington's simple birthplace farm, the drive arrives at Lee's birthplace, the manorial Stratford Hall. Continuing to the tip of the neck, you can hop a ferry and travel halfway across the Chesapeake Bay to memorable Tangier Island. The community of bay watermen here continue a lifestyle little changed over the last century.

Antique store, Fredericksburg

Begin in ❶ **Fredericksburg★** *(Visitor Center, 706 Caroline St. 540-373-1776 or 800-678-4748),* whose quaint colonial downtown slopes toward the muddy Rappahannock. Its pleasant brick storefronts now house a bevy of cafés, boutiques, antique shops, and historic sites. The former town hall/market house (1816) makes a good starting point, as it has been transformed into the **Fredericksburg Area Museum and Cultural Center** *(907 Princess Anne St. 540-371-3037. Adm. fee)*, with exhibits related to the region's rich past and artistic present. As early as 1728, this strategic town at the fall line of the Rappahannock was founded as a tobacco port. It remained a hub of trade and industry throughout the century, manufacturing munitions during the Revolution. Buildings scattered throughout town attest to the port's colonial prominence.

At the **Rising Sun Tavern** *(1304 Caroline St. 540-371-1494. Adm. fee)*, mop-capped "wenches" escort visitors on a guided tour of the inviting hostelry, now a museum. The structure was originally built in 1760 as the private home of Charles Washington, George's brother. George and his siblings spent much of their childhood at nearby Ferry Farm (see page 70), and the region boasts many Washington family associations.

Costumed guide, Rising Sun Tavern

The **Hugh Mercer Apothecary Shop** *(1020 Caroline St. 540-373-3362. Adm. fee)* was established by Washington's friend Hugh Mercer. Drawers and shelves from the original apothecary are included in the period decor.

The dormered, brick **James Monroe Museum** *(908 Charles St. 540-899-4559. Adm. fee)* commemorates the nation's fifth President. The museum houses the largest collection of Monroe-related materials in the country, including the French directoire-style desk on which Monroe penned his 1823 annual message to Congress, outlining what came to be known as the Monroe Doctrine.

If the 18th century was kind to Fredericksburg, the 19th was cruel. Its strategic location quickly became a liability as the Civil War engulfed Virginia. Lying equidistant from the Federal capital of Washington, D.C., and the Confederate capital of Richmond, the town was mauled in battle after battle. The **Fredericksburg & Spotsylvania National Military Park★★** *(Main Visitor Center, 1013 Lafayette Blvd. 540-373-6122)* comprises several historic structures and four major battlefields in the area: Fredericksburg (December 1862), Chancellorsville (May 1863), the Wilderness

(May 1864), and Spotsylvania Court House (May 1864). The earliest battle took place at Marye's Heights in the bitter December cold of 1862. Preparing for a Union attack, Lee's men had secured this high ground overlooking the town. Watching the gathering Union forces, Lee uttered, "It is well that war is so terrible—we should grow too fond of it." His words were prophetic: When the Federals advanced, they were slaughtered in horrific droves.

To visit the 2 **Chancellorsville** site, head west on Va. 3. About 10 miles from Fredericksburg, a museum and driving tour through the woods interpret the battle at Chancellorsville, where the South scored a brilliant victory at great cost. Stonewall Jackson, Lee's "right arm," was mistakenly shot by Southern riflemen here and died of his wounds eight days later (see sidebar page 72).

Head back to town on Va. 3 and cross the Rappahannock to **Chatham** *(120 Chatham Ln. 540-371-0802),* a historic 18th-century house open to public view. At various stages of the war, Union officers headquartered here while planning their attacks on nearby Fredericksburg. Like many such houses, this one also served as a Union hospital, and both Clara Barton and Walt Whitman nursed the wounded here.

From Chatham continue south on Va. 3 and watch for the turnoff to **Ferry Farm** *(540-372-4487. Mon.-Fri.; adm. fee),* where George Washington spent much of his boyhood. Though he founded a dynasty of well-heeled Virginians, his own upbringing on this farm across the river from Fredericksburg was less than extravagant; no buildings from his era remain.

Moving through farm country edged by stands of oak

Washington Slept Here

Fredericksburg's genteel south side holds two Washington family homes. In 1772 George purchased the small clapboard, now called the **Mary Washington House** *(1200 Charles St. 540-373-1569. Adm. fee),* for his mother, and it still holds her personal effects. He situated his mother near his only sister, Betty Lewis, whose grand Georgian home, **Kenmore Plantation and Gardens** *(1201 Washington Ave. 540-373-3381. Adm. fee),* was once the heart of a large plantation that sprawled across 13,000 acres. Kenmore now lies on a few shaded acres in the middle of a residential neighborhood, but its dignity remains intact. Period furnishings recall the colonial high style, and the house is famous for the ornate plasterwork that decorates its ceilings, created by an anonymous craftsmen remembered only as the "stucco man."

Chancellorsville section, Fredericksburg & Spotsylvania National Military Park

At George Washington Birthplace National Monument

and pine, the drive moseys across the almost unbroken ruralness of the Northern Neck, passing on its way through Westmoreland County, where James Monroe was born. After about 40 miles, the drive arrives at the 3 **George Washington Birthplace National Monument** *(Off Va. 3 on Va. 204. 804-224-1732. Adm. fee),* unmistakable for the small replica of the Washington Monument obelisk that suddenly appears as you clear a bluff on Va. 204. In 1732 the father of our country was born here to Augustine and Mary Ball Washington. The languid, cedar-rimmed setting on the banks of Popes Creek contains no original buildings, as the family home burned during the Revolutionary War. But a colonial revival "memorial house" from the 1930s now re-creates the life of a prosperous, but not wealthy, planter in the first half of the 18th century. The Park Service administers the grounds as a working farm, with costumed interpreters, livestock, and kitchen gardens.

Return to Va. 3 and continue just a few miles farther down the neck to the intersection with Va. 214. This leads to the birthplace of another state luminary, Robert E. Lee. Far from the humble colonial surroundings of Washington's infancy, 4 **Stratford Hall**★ *(Va. 214. 804-493-8038. Adm. fee)* exudes the long breeding of a Virginia dynasty. The H-shaped brick mansion, with its massive chimney clusters, was the ancestral home of the Lee family. Thomas Lee built the house in the 1730s and his six sons all became major players in the fight for independence. John Adams called them "this band of brothers, intrepid and unchangeable, who . . . stood in the gap, in defense of their country." Both Richard Henry and Francis Lightfoot Lee signed the Declaration of Independence.

Light Horse Harry Lee, a famous cavalry commander

in the Revolution, married a Lee cousin in April 1782 and occupied the house. When Matilda, his first wife, died, he married Anne Hill Carter, who in 1807 gave birth to a son, Robert Edward, at Stratford. But the boy would spend only four years here before his father's bad business investments put the family in financial straits.

Resembling a British country manor, the house is centered around an enormous paneled Great Hall, but the most compelling room is the southeast bedroom where Lee was born and his crib still stands. A greensward sweeps down from the house to the distant Potomac and a reconstructed mill grinds grains into flours.

From Stratford Hall, Va. 3 turns sharply south and soon bends through the softly shaded streets of Montross. In the town of Warsaw, the drive turns east on US 360 and heads for the longtime fishing port of **Reedville.** A fleet of menhaden trawlers use this small town as a base, but most travelers come here to take the 1.5-hour cruise to legendary 5 **Tangier Island**★ *(Tangier and Rappahannock Cruises 804-453-2628. May–mid-Oct.; fare).* Floating almost in the middle of the Chesapeake Bay, this small 3.5-mile-long island preserves a living but lapsing culture—that of the bay's watermen. Along its protected boat channel, small white sheds, "soft-shell crab plantations," are cantilevered out over the water, and flat-bottomed deadrises, long the waterman's vehicle of choice, bob nearby. The town's narrow lanes edge past tidy houses and across marshes where reed grasses wave in the perpetual wind off the bay. For a taste of the seafood harvested here—and the distinctive Elizabethan-derived dialect the islanders still maintain—stop at **Hilda Crockett's Chesapeake House** *(16243 Main Ridge Rd. 804-891-2331. Mid-April–mid-Oct.).* Sitting at a long communal table, you can fill up on a family-style meal of fresh vegetables, crab cakes, clam fritters, potato salad, and lots of small-town bonhomie.

The Indomitable Stonewall

Eccentric, enigmatic, God-fearing, and one of America's most brilliant military strategists, Thomas Jonathan "Stonewall" Jackson was mistakenly shot by Confederate riflemen at Chancellorsville in May 1863. His arm amputated, Jackson was taken to the nearby Chandler plantation to recover. He did not. When the troops in the field heard of his death, "a great sob swept over the Army," one observer wrote. "It was the heartbreak of the Southern Confederacy." The plantation office where he died, now part of the Fredericksburg & Spotsylvania N.M.P., is preserved as the **Stonewall Jackson Shrine** *(Rte. 606 south of Fredericksburg. 804-633-6076. Daily in summer; call for off-season hours).*

Workboat, Tangier Island

Along the James ★★

● 135 miles ● 3 to 4 days ● Year-round

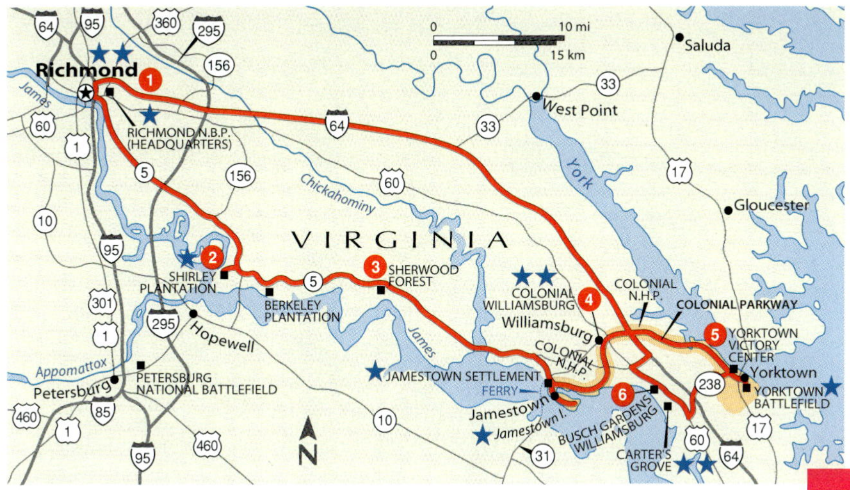

The James River might aptly be called the Nile of Virginia, for its wide brown waters have spawned much of the Old Dominion's modern civilization. This drive rambles south along the river's edge, beginning at its fall line in Richmond—once the Confederate and now the state capital—and continuing downriver, past the colonial plantations that have housed Virginia gentry for more than 350 years. Near Jamestown, the drive loops around the little island where English settlers first established a tentative toehold. The route then cuts inland along the Colonial Parkway to Williamsburg. Here, colonial restoration has become an art form and the town's 18th-century demeanor depicts life on the eve of Revolution. Continuing east, the parkway ends at the redoubts and ridges of the Yorktown battlefields, where the reality of a colonial victory became manifest. Before returning to Richmond, you can reconnect with the 20th century on the high-tech, hair-raising rides at Busch Gardens.

Linden Row, Richmond

The drive begins in 1 **Richmond★★** *(Visitor Center 804-358-5511 or 888-RICHMOND),* a city that is many things to many people. To descendants of the Old South it will be forever remembered as the capital of the Confederacy, steeped in the gallantry of Lee, Jackson, Davis, and Stuart. To younger Virginians and to casual visitors, Richmond is a city on the move—a Fortune 500 favorite, and a center of museums, cafés, universities, and Southern-style urbanity.

Sunday best on Monument Avenue

The old downtown embodies both of these Richmonds. Once the shopping destination of the upper South, its core has fallen into decrepitude, despite repeated attempts at revitalization. But the downtown's eastern side claims a multitude of memorable sites. The columned and domed **Virginia State Capitol★** *(9th and Broad Sts. 804-786-4344),* designed by Thomas Jefferson in his best neoclassic hand, dominates a grassy green knoll. Beneath the capitol's rotunda stands a marble statue of George Washington, modeled from life by French sculptor Jean-Antoine Houdon. Surrounding Washington are the seven other Virginians who served as U.S. Presidents, as well his Revolutionary ally, the Marquis de Lafayette—all represented in wall-niche busts. It was in the capitol's House of Delegates that Robert E. Lee received his appointment as head of Virginia's Confederate forces and that the dashing Aaron Burr was tried for treason.

Future Supreme Court Chief Justice John Marshall heard the Burr treason case as a circuit court judge. Marshall, a lover of sports who disliked pretense, led a homespun life in the ample, simple brick house now open to the public as the **John Marshall House** *(818 E. Marshall St. 804-648-7998. Tues.-Sat.; adm. fee).*

There is nothing unpretentious about the nearby **White House of the Confederacy** *(1201 E. Clay St. 804-649-1861. Adm. fee),* the flowery, red-brocade festooned Victorian where Jefferson Davis lived with his family and served as doomed president of the South from 1861 to 1865. In the same complex, the **Museum of the Confederacy** displays the personal effects of such Confederate Army notables as

Robert E. Lee and Jeb Stuart. Its comprehensive collection includes battle flags, weaponry, and paintings relating to the war.

An enlightened portrait of antebellum Richmond can be found up the street at the **Valentine Museum★** *(1015 E. Clay St. 804-649-0711. Adm. fee).* This renowned archival repository also mounts wonderful exhibits on the many lives and changing times of this city, and its adjacent 1812 **Wickham House** takes an innovative, upstairs-downstairs approach to interpretation. As you walk through the finely appointed rooms, you can hear recorded, simulated dialogues between slaves, the Wickhams, and their visitors—an affecting oral drama of the interrelated lives of antebellum Richmond. A gem of refined federal taste, the house is well-known for its elegantly cantilevered spiral staircase and rare neoclassic wall paintings.

Much of the city's warehouse district was burned by Confederates at the end of the war, to keep it out of the hands of the advancing Union Army. Some buildings that did survive are now part of the city's up-and-coming **Shockoe Slip** *(13th and Cary Sts.),* whose restaurants and boutiques make it the city's liveliest nightspot. During the day, the nearby **Farmers Market** *(17th and Main Sts.),* housed in the turreted old redbrick railroad station, offers a colorful concoction of fresh produce and claims to be the oldest continuously operating market in the country.

A memorial to Richmond's greatest literary figure stands

Robert E. Lee memorial on Monument Avenue, Richmond

nearby. The **Edgar Allan Poe Museum** *(1914-16 E. Main St. 804-648-5523. Adm. fee)* poignantly details, in memorabilia and writings, the tragic life of the poet and author. Poe's mother, an acclaimed actress, died when he was two, and the boy was raised by foster parents in Richmond. The museum occupies the Old Stone House, the city's oldest residential dwelling, built between 1737 and 1740.

Virginia Museum of Fine Arts, Richmond

Poe's mother, Elizabeth Arnold Poe, is buried along with George Wythe and other prominent Virginians in the nearby cemetery of **St. John's Church** *(2401 E. Broad St. 804-648-5015).* The large white-frame church has witnessed a lot of history, including Patrick Henry's famous proclamation to his fellow Virginia delegates in 1775, that he wanted "liberty . . . or death."

Nearby is **Chimborazo Hill,** well known to Civil War enthusiasts. It was here that the Confederacy maintained the world's largest hospital during the 1860s, treating some 76,000 casualties of the war. The rambling tents and shacks of the makeshift hospital are long gone, but the Park Service maintains headquarters here for the **Richmond National Battlefield Park★** *(3215 E. Broad St. 804-226-1981),* a complex of ten Civil War sites scattered through the city's outskirts. A lengthy driving tour connects these infamous killing fields, which include Gaines's Mill, Malvern Hill, and Cold Harbor.

Richmond suffered terribly during the war, and near the war's end, in the face of advancing Union troops, Southern forces set fire to its warehouses, burning much of the city. Slowly, the old capital recovered the refinement and grace it possessed before the conflict. One site that speaks volumes about Richmond's turn-of-the-century grandeur is the historic old **Jefferson Hotel** *(Franklin and Adams Sts. 804-788-8000 or 800-424-8014),* at the west edge of downtown. The towered, Italianate extravaganza, built in 1895, boasts its own splendid rotunda, ringed by massive faux-marble columns and an ornate mezzanine and overhung by a stained-glass skylight. In the lobby, another stained-glass skylight, this one by Tiffany, arcs above a statue of Thomas Jefferson sculptured by Virginian Edward Valentine.

A few blocks beyond the hotel, Franklin Street turns into the city's most famous thoroughfare, **Monument Avenue.** Robert E. Lee, Jefferson Davis, Stonewall Jackson, and Jeb Stuart are all honored with statues along this broad gracious boulevard, fronted by dignified Victorian houses. Monument Avenue intersects the Boulevard, where two superb museums are situated within a block of one another. The **Virginia Historical Society★** *(428 N. Boulevard. 804-358-4901. Adm. fee),* once a library and research facility, now features innovative changing exhibits on different aspects of state history, from a reinterpretation of Pocahontas to Virginia in the 1950s. The society has wisely preserved its Cheek Gallery, whose romantic murals honor Southern heroism in the Civil War.

The impressive holdings of the **Virginia Museum of Fine Arts★★** *(Boulevard and Grove Ave. 804-367-0844. Donation),* one of the region's finest art museums, are displayed in several wings—Classical, African, European, American, and Contemporary. The collections range from Egyptian and Greek artifacts to Impressionist and Postimpressionist works. Particularly outstanding are its collection of gem-encrusted Fabergé Imperial Easter Eggs and its galleries of art nouveau and art deco pieces.

The **Science Museum of Virginia** *(2500 W. Broad St. 804-367-6552. Adm. fee)* is appealing to both kids and adults. The columned and domed structure, designed by John Russell Pope in 1916 and for years the Broad Street Station railroad terminal, is now filled with user-friendly, interactive ways to explore such intriguing subjects as chemistry, physics, and astronomy.

Flight simulator, Science Museum of Virginia

The wealthy of an earlier era dotted the outlying reaches of Richmond with sumptuous estates. Do not miss the 1890s **Maymont★** *(1700 Hampton St. 804-358-7166. Tues.-Sun.; donation),* a turreted Gilded Age extravaganza in stone. The Romanesque Revival exterior belies a surprisingly intimate interior, where the rooms are still decorated with the furnishings of James and Sallie May Dooley. Sallie's boudoir attests to the fantasies that money can buy—an elaborate, carved swan bed and a Tiffany-designed dressing table of silver and carved narwhal tusks. The house tops a knoll that falls away past Italian fountains, wisteria-entwined arches, and Japanese gardens, where whiffs of the Gilded Age linger.

More floral splendor can be found at the **Lewis Ginter Botanical Garden** *(Lakeside Ave. at Hilliard Rd. 804-262-9887. Adm. fee),* whose 80-some acres are vibrant with such Virginia favorites as daffodils, daylilies, azaleas, and rhododendrons. Before leaving this city, drive through the 300-acre campus of the **University of Richmond** *(Patterson Ave. and Three Chopt Rd.),* ranked among the most beautiful in the country. The university's Gothic stone halls, centered around a large lake, make a pleasant break from Virginia's abundance of neoclassic architecture.

Leave Richmond on Va. 5 east, the "plantation route." Twisting through farm fields, it follows the James River past a collection of the finest colonial plantations in the country *(For general information, call 804-829-5121).* About 20 miles outside Richmond, you'll see a sign for the first of them.

2 **Shirley Plantation★** *(804-829-5121 or 800-232-1613. Adm. fee)* lays claim to being the oldest plantation in America, settled in 1613 and still farmed. Working fields surround the stately Queen Anne manor house, with its two-story neoclassic verandas, hipped roof, and massive chimneys. Built in the 1720s by a member of the baronial Carter clan, the house has remained home to the Hill-Carter family to the present day; most of its 18th- and 19th-century furnishings are family pieces. Three stories above the large entrance hall floats the house's famous square-rigged, or flying, staircase. The only one in this country, it was based on similar designs by English architect Christopher Wren. Tours are exceptionally informative, covering the family's deep tentacles in state history. Robert E. Lee's mother, Anne Hill Carter, was born at Shirley and married Revolutionary War hero Light Horse Harry Lee here.

Several miles down Va. 5, signs lead to another house drenched in history, **Berkeley Plantation** *(12602 Harrison Landing Rd. 804-829-6018. Adm. fee),* home of the Harrison family. Both Benjamin Harrison, signer of the Declaration of Independence, and William Henry Harrison, the ninth President, were born in this 1726 redbrick Georgian, and

Plantation Labor

The vast Virginia plantations established in the 17th and 18th centuries were almost self-sufficient fiefdoms. Typically, they made their own brick, ground their own grain, spun enough cloth, and produced enough food for their scores of slaves and indentured servants. The ultimate goal was to grow and cure the "jovial weed" that made the planters rich. Tobacco was a cruel master, so hard on the land that after only three or four harvests, the soil was played out. Early planters relied on indentured servants for labor to plant, tend, and pick tobacco. By the late 1600s, it became difficult to attract European labor, and the use of slave labor became firmly entrenched. Before slavery ended, 11 million Africans had been enslaved and forced across the ocean to work in the fields of the New World.

Shirley Plantation, along the James River

the 23rd President, Benjamin Harrison, considered it his ancestral home. But the land here had already earned historic status before their tenure, when a group of Englishmen celebrated the first Thanksgiving down by the James in 1619. During the Civil War, Union Maj. Gen. George McClellan also used the riverfront here as his headquarters during the 1862 Peninsula Campaign to take Richmond. During that period the Army's bugled lullaby, "Taps," was composed on the grounds. In one of history's strange twists, the current owner of the mansion is the son of McClellan's drummer boy. He and his wife have lovingly restored the house and filled it with 18th- and 19th-century antiques. Five terraced gardens, dug by hand before the Revolutionary War, lead out from the house to the James River.

Yet another President is associated with the mansions along the James. Some 10 miles down Va. 5 stands the 300-foot-long white clapboard to which President John Tyler retired after his term in the White House (1841-1845). Known as the longest frame house in America, 3 **Sherwood Forest** *(804-829-2947. Adm. fee)* has a lighthearted, mid-19th-century ebullience, probably owing to the tastes of Tyler's young bride, Julia Gardiner Tyler.

Continue on Va. 5 to its junction with Rte. 614 (Greensprings Road) and follow signs to Jamestown.

Jamestown Island★ *(Colonial National Historical Park 757-229-1733. Adm. fee)* seems an unlikely spot for the founding of a colonial settlement. Quiet now reigns in this star-crossed area, where gentle breezes off the James sway the tall pines edging the small island's marshlands. Visitor Center exhibits explain the hardships that Englishmen and women endured here from 1607 until 1699, when the town was more or less abandoned and the colonial capital moved inland to Williamsburg. Today, brick outlines mark the foundations of James Cittie, and a commanding statue of the redoubtable John Smith, whose fortitude saw the first band of colonists through to survival, watches over the townsite. An old brick church tower is the only piece of the past still standing on the 1,500-acre island, but recent excavations have uncovered the adjacent site of the original 1607 James Fort. Looping through the rest of the wooded island, an interpretive drive gives a keen sense of the hope and glory that began and ended here.

Re-created thatched houses, Jamestown Settlement

Just on the other side of the causeway that connects the island to the mainland, the National Park Service has re-created a 1608 glasshouse. Working with glowing molten globs, latter-day craftsmen in knee breeches blow the shapeless lumps into pitchers, glasses, and other colonial-appropriate items.

At **Jamestown Settlement★** *(Colonial Pkwy. 757-253-4838. Adm. fee)* the state has gone to elaborate lengths in interpreting the life of both colonists and Native Americans in 17th-century Virginia. A palisaded fort and Indian village stand on the grounds, and on the riverfront visitors can board replicas of the three ships—the *Susan Constant, Godspeed,* and *Discovery*—that landed nearby in 1607. Expansive indoor exhibits describe Jamestown's origins in England, the colony's first century, and the culture of Virginia's Powhatan Indians.

From Jamestown, the wide, graceful ribbon of the Colonial Parkway sweeps past marshes and through woodlands on its way to 4 **Colonial Williamsburg★★** *(Visitor Center accessible from Colonial Pkwy. 757-229-1000 or 800-HISTORY. General adm. fee covers most historic buildings and museums; overall site and some re-created buildings free).* This probably ranks as one of the most exhaustively researched and interpreted historic sites in the world, thanks in large part to John D. Rockefeller, Jr. Encouraged by a local clergyman, W.A.R. Goodwin, Rockefeller began restoring buildings in the somewhat dilapidated town in the 1920s. Today, the 173-acre complex re-creates the colonial capital that existed here for most of the 1700s. A living history mecca that draws visitors from throughout the world, the town consists of 88 original buildings and hundreds of replicated structures—all carefully researched and constructed on their original foundations.

Though the town lacks the noisy, noisome, mud-spattered boisterousness it boasted in its colonial heyday, it is, in most other ways, admirably authentic. The costumed interpreters stationed in the historic buildings are exceedingly well-versed and paint a clear picture of conditions here in the 1770s, when patriots like Thomas Jefferson, George Washington, and Patrick Henry locked horns with the royal authorities and ultimately opted for revolution. Duke of Gloucester Street, virtually all of which is a pedestrian thoroughfare, serves as the town axis, running about a mile from the College of William and Mary to the Capitol.

Aboard the re-created *Susan Constant*

The reconstructed brick **Capitol★** reflects in its H shape the design of colonial government. The popularly elected representatives met on one side in the rather simple surroundings of the Hall of the House of Burgesses. It was from the benches of this chamber that revolution sprouted and Patrick Henry rose to proclaim that "Caesar … had his Brutus, Charles the First his Cromwell, and George the Third may profit by their example." Across the piazza, on the other side of the building, royal interests reigned. In the lower-level courtroom, the General Court met and meted out punishment to wrongdoers, sending some to the abysmal brick gaol located next door. On the upper level, amid fine appointments, the Governor's Council (consisting of 12 prominent colonists appointed by the king), met and, in tandem with the House of Burgesses, passed the laws of the land. For some 150 years this more or less orderly form of colonial government prevailed, but increasing tensions with Britain came to a head in 1774, when the royal government dissolved the treasonous House of Burgesses, who, undaunted, reconvened in nearby **Raleigh Tavern.**

Also a reconstruction, the tavern, perhaps more than any other building, reflects the rambunctious enthusiasm early visitors to this city, one of the few urban centers in the colony, would have experienced. Bedchambers were crammed with boarders, and tailors sold their wares from side rooms. On the main level, large halls served as meeting places and ballrooms; billiards were played at a massive table in a back room and gentlemen tried their hand at whist nearby.

Duke of Gloucester Street, Colonial Williamsburg

The 18th-century urban swirl of Williamsburg is obvious from the many small businesses—shoemakers, apothecaries, taverns, metalsmiths—that stand chockablock along Duke of Gloucester Street. Now, as then, the wares in many shops are for sale.

A long greensward announces the unmistakable grandeur of the **Governor's Palace★.** The original palace, completed in 1722 and improved on periodically, burned to the ground in 1781 while being used as a hospital for Colonials wounded in the fighting at Yorktown. The current structure, occupying the original foundations, is distinguished by elegant woodworking and appointments. Especially impressive are the decorative arrangements of firearms, hung on walls and ceilings as embellishments.

Near the palace are two private homes now open to the public, their stories integral to the history of Williamsburg. The capacious clapboard **Peyton Randolph House** *(Nicholson and N. England Sts.)* embodies the life of prominent lawyer Randolph, who presided over the First and Second Continental Congresses in Philadelphia. Some historians contend he would have been a logical choice for first President, had he lived through the war. The **George Wythe House,** a plain-faced Georgian brick structure fronting the Palace Green, hosted many promising young visitors, from Thomas Jefferson to John Marshall. Wythe, a jurist and teacher of law at William and Mary, mentored these men, and through them exercised a deep influence on the system of law and government that eventually developed in the new republic. Jefferson called Wythe his "most affectionate friend through life."

Capitol, Colonial Williamsburg

Though some of these colonial intellectuals expressed doubts about organized religion, the Anglican Church nonetheless enjoyed the backing of royal authority. White Virginians were required to attend services once a month, and in this town that meant attending **Bruton Parish Church.** It still stands just beyond the Wythe house, its walled graveyard protecting tilting, weather-worn headstones. The current brick church, small but elegant, took shape from 1712 to 1715 and has been in use ever since.

As you edge toward the **College of William and Mary** *(804-221-2630),* pristine colonialism gives way to the energy of student life. Commercial shops and restaurants cluster at this end of Duke of Gloucester Street, anchored by the perfect brick symmetry of the college's **Wren Building★.** In 1693 King William III and Queen Mary II chartered the college, to ensure that solid Anglican beliefs

Yorktown Battlefield

were perpetuated on American soil. Two years later the foundations for the Wren Building were laid and have withstood time. Enlarged, damaged by fire, and repaired often in its long life, the Wren is the oldest academic building in continuous use in America. Bare, late 17th-century-style classrooms fill the interior, along with a lovely chapel and a Great Hall that served as a common dining room. Two Georgian structures flank the Wren: the **Brafferton** (1723) and the **President's House** (1732). The eminent English scientist Robert Boyle funded the former, as a school for Native Americans.

A reconstruction of the **Public Hospital** *(S. Henry and Francis Sts.)* that housed the mentally ill from 1773 until it was destroyed by fire in 1885, now houses exhibits tracing the evolution of treatment for patients afflicted with mental illnesses. In addition, ingenious modern architect Kevin Roche has utilized the hospital as an entryway to an essentially underground museum, the **DeWitt Wallace Decorative Arts Gallery★.** Here, room after room displays world-class decorative arts relating to the colonial period: furniture by American master craftsmen, porcelains, and paintings of such note as Charles Willson Peale's military portrait of a young Washington. A compellingly contemplative garden honors Lila Acheson Wallace, benefactor of the museum and cofounder with her husband, DeWitt, of *Reader's Digest*.

The nearby **Abby Aldrich Rockefeller Folk Art Center★★** *(Off Francis St. on S. England St.)* contains

perhaps the finest American folk art collection in the world. Old favorites such as a rendition of Edward Hick's "Peaceable Kingdom" and the anonymous but superb "Baby in Red Chair" capture the naive beauty of early American art.

From Williamsburg, the Colonial Parkway tunnels southeast through forests before reaching the banks of the York River. Exhibits at the 5 **Yorktown Victory Center** *(Colonial Pkwy. and Va. 238. 757-253-4838. Adm. fee)* chronicle the American Revolution from the beginnings of colonial unrest to the formation of a new nation and the adoption of the Constitution and Bill of Rights. Themed galleries feature the accounts of diverse individuals who lived during the Revolution and tell of "Yorktown's Sunken Fleet," ships lost during the 1781 Siege of Yorktown. On the grounds of the complex, tents and cabins peopled by living history interpreters re-create a Continental Army encampment and an 18th-century farm.

The siege is recounted in vivid detail at the **Yorktown Battlefield★** *(South end of Colonial Pkwy. 757-898-3400),* where a Visitor Center offers exhibits, movies, and a self-guided driving tour that leads past historic sites. For nine days in the early fall of 1781, Washington pummeled Cornwallis's army here, until at last the British general called for a surrender parley. The parties met at the **Moore House,** and on October 19, the armies—all but the arrogant Cornwallis—met on **Surrender Field.** As the redcoats piped out "The World Turned Upside Down," the Americans accepted the British defeat. Though the war lingered on for two more years, the decisive victory at Yorktown proved to be the straw that broke the back of the empire.

Hollyhock at Carter's Grove

Hardly the extravaganza that is Williamsburg, **Yorktown** has perhaps a more poignant appeal as it is still very much a lived-in town. In the early 18th century, it thrived as a seaport with quick access to the Chesapeake Bay and thence the Atlantic. Today the quiet Main Street is still dotted with buildings from that colonial boom time, including the oldest **customhouse** in the country and the dignified 1730 **Nelson House** *(Main St. 757-898-3400).* Thomas Nelson, Jr., a signer of the Declaration of Independence and Revolutionary War commander, ordered this, his own house, shelled during the siege, as British were believed to be headquartered here. One of his cannonballs is still lodged in the walls. Along with the house, Nelson lost most of his fortune in the Revolution. He lies in the cemetery of diminutive **Grace Church** (1697). Only in this century was a grave marker added over the patriot's remains. On the banks above the river the imposing **Yorktown Victory Monument,** topped by Victory with her arms outstretched, celebrates the success at Yorktown.

Return to the Yorktown Victory Center and turn left on Va. 238 for about 8 miles, then right on US 60 to **Carter's Grove★★** *(757-229-1000 or 800-HISTORY. March-Dec.; adm. fee).* Facing the James, the central portion of the grand brick edifice was constructed by a descendant of 17th-century land baron Robert "King" Carter. During the 1930s, when the colonial revival movement was at its zenith, the impressive, hipped-roof Georgian manor was purchased by the McCreas, whose railroad and tobacco wealth brought the house to its present state of grandeur.

Cyclone ride, Busch Gardens Williamsburg

On the fields that sweep below the house toward the river, archaeologists have uncovered **Wolstenholme Towne,** one of the early palisaded town forts built by the English. A reconstructed tower and outlines of the fort have been put in place, with audio tapes aiding the experience. More detailed exhibits and artifacts from the dig, including a superb helmet, are featured in the adjacent **Winthrop Rockefeller Archaeology Museum.** The grounds also include a cluster of re-created slave quarters, where guides explain that life on an 18th-century Virginia plantation was far from grand for all its inhabitants.

From Carter's Grove, US 60 west will bring you to **6 Busch Gardens Williamsburg** *(804-253-3350. Late May–late Oct.; adm. fee).* Anheuser-Busch puts a historic spin on 20th-century theme-park fun here, and live shows and action rides are scattered through nine 17th-century-style European villages set amid well-landscaped grounds.

Take I-64 west for 55 miles to return to Richmond.

The Tidewater

● 120 miles ● 2 days ● Spring through fall

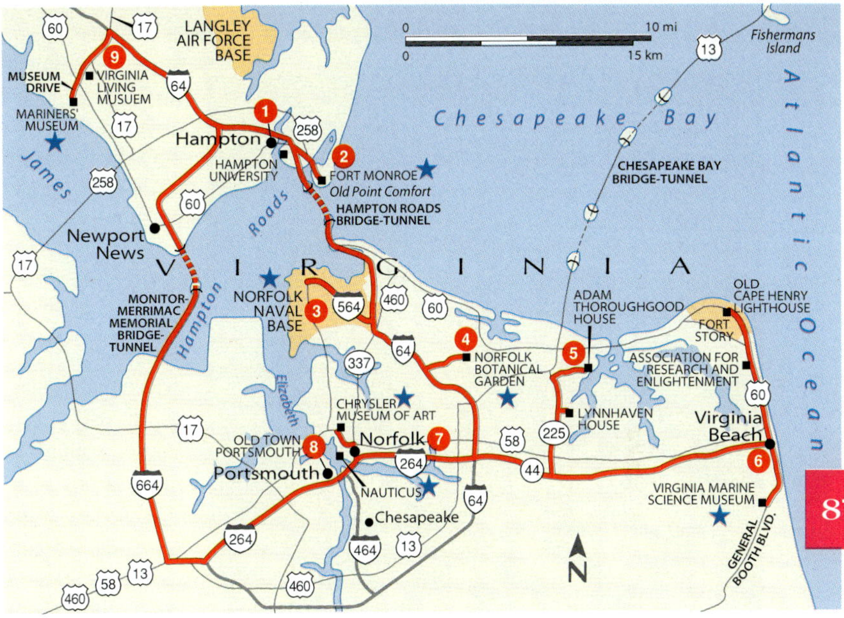

Marshes, rivers, and meandering creeks filigree this low-country tideland, where water has long defined the doings of man. The fertile, shallow water known as the Chesapeake Bay empties into the Atlantic here, and both seafood-harvesting watermen and committed military industrialists have made good use of these waters. Hampton, where the drive takes off, has a lively history, beginning with the early colonists and marching straight into the space age. In Norfolk, on the other side of Hampton Roads, the drive stops at Norfolk Naval Base, the largest such base in the world, before heading for the Atlantic. In the state's great ocean resort, Virginia Beach, high-rise hotels stand shoulder-to-shoulder above wide white sands. Turning inland toward Norfolk, Portsmouth, and Newport News, the drive visits the homes of pioneering 18th-century entrepreneurs and museums that celebrate art, the area's marine realms, mariners, and military heroes.

Amphibious command ship, Norfolk Naval Base

Begin your tour in ❶ **Hampton** *(Visitor Center, 710 Settlers Landing Rd. 757-727-1102 or 800-800-2202),* which proudly bills itself as the oldest continuous English-speaking settlement in America. While it does date from the early colonial period (1610), Hampton has experienced a lot of history since then and now comprises an eclectic mix of its many pasts. Infused with a slow-moving Southern style, the town was actually a Union bastion during the Civil War and a center of the incipient space age a century later, when early NASA astronauts trained here at Langley Air Force Base. The sleepy little downtown recalls all these elements. In the quietude of **St. John's Episcopal Church** *(100 W. Queens Way. 757-722-2567)* old gravestones pace the centuries. The Georgian brick church (1728) was badly damaged in two fires that swept the town—one in the War of 1812 and another in the Civil War, but it rose like a phoenix from both conflagrations. Its Victorian interior is still streaked with light from a stained-glass window depicting Pocahontas, and the church's English Communion silver dates from 1618, making it the oldest in continual use in this country.

Virginia Beach

Along the waterfront nearby the tone changes dramatically with the soaring glass-and-brick **Virginia Air and Space Center★** *(600 Settlers Landing Rd. 757-727-0900 or 800-296-0800. Adm. fee).* Completed in 1992, the official

Visitor Center for the NASA Langley Research Center overlooks the working docks of Hampton River. Inside the museum, exhibits trace the history of Hampton Roads from its founding as a colonial port to its glory days as home to the astronauts. Legendary aircraft dangle from the building's high recesses, but the great draw is the Apollo 12 Command Module that ferried those first pioneers to the moon. An IMAX theater brings the experience of air travel vividly to life.

Across the narrow river, the green sloping banks of **Hampton University** *(757-727-5308)* are shaded by venerable trees and 19th-century redbrick halls. The university's roots go back to the Hampton Normal and Agricultural Institute, founded by abolitionists who came south to educate the many former slaves that congregated around Union-held Fort Monroe. At the lovely **Memorial Chapel,** designed in the 1880s, you can sit in pine pews hewed by the students themselves. Rambling **Virginia Hall** also enjoys architectural esteem as the work of Richard Morris Hunt. A small **museum** *(757-727-5308)* houses African, African-American, and Native American artifacts. The institute's most renowned student was Booker T. Washington. Born into slavery in central Virginia and freed as a boy by the Emancipation Proclamation, he became a leading black spokesman and founder of Alabama's Tuskegee Institute.

From the windswept tip of Hampton's Old Point Comfort, 2 **Fort Monroe★** *(End of Va. 258)* has guarded the entrance to Hampton Roads from the Chesapeake Bay since 1819. Although this once mighty military bastion no longer performs its original mission, it is more than a gracious anachronism—it houses the Army's Training and Doctrine Command. The old irregular polygonal-shaped moated fortress, with its sod roofs, contains the **Casemate Museum** *(757-727-3391),* where exhibits recount the area's long military history: how the fort—the Gibraltar of the Chesapeake—was part of

Virginia Marine Science Museum, Virginia Beach

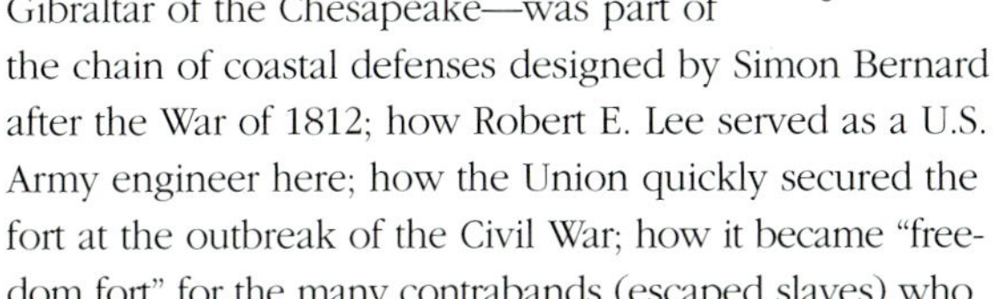

the chain of coastal defenses designed by Simon Bernard after the War of 1812; how Robert E. Lee served as a U.S. Army engineer here; how the Union quickly secured the fort at the outbreak of the Civil War; how it became "freedom fort" for the many contrabands (escaped slaves) who flocked here; and how Confederate President Jefferson Davis was imprisoned in a small casemate here after the war. Inside the original fort, antebellum houses recall the days when Lee lived here happily with his young family in what is now Quarters Number 17. The most imposing of the houses, **Quarters Number One,** sheltered such distinguished guests as the Marquis de Lafayette, King David Kalakaua of Hawaii, and Abraham Lincoln. Just beyond the moat, the **Old Point Comfort Lighthouse** (1802) stares out into Chesapeake Bay.

For a look at 20th-century naval warfare capabilities, take the Hampton Roads Bridge-Tunnel (I-64) east and follow signs for the 3 **Norfolk Naval Base**★ *(Naval base tour and info. Hampton Blvd. at Gate 5. 757-444-7955. Tours originate here; call for hours).* Harbored along a spit of land lying between the Elizabeth River and Willoughby Bay, this is the largest naval complex in the world. Its 8 miles of waterfront is home port to roughly a hundred ships—subs, destroyers, tenders, aircraft carriers, and on and on—as well as some 71,000 military and 16,000 civilian personnel.

Return to I-64 and follow exit signs for the 4 **Norfolk Botanical Garden**★ *(Azalea Garden Rd. near the Norfolk airport. 757-441-5830. Adm. fee),* whose 155 acres are covered in the languid, lovely flora of coastal Virginia. Paths thread through dense shadow patches of pine, camellia, holly, and rhododendron, but the true glory of this garden is its azaleas. They're honored each April during the International Azalea Festival, which in turn celebrates, believe it or not, the North Atlantic Treaty Organization (NATO).

Farther along the drive, the early human life of this area survives in two historic settings. The **Lynnhaven House** *(4405 Wishart Rd. 757-664-6200. Call for hours; adm. fee),* a simple cottage, dates from 1725 and celebrates the hardihood of farmers in that era. The 5 **Adam Thoroughgood House** *(1636 Parrish Rd. 757-664-6200. Jan.-March Tues.-Sat., April-Dec. Tues.-Sun.; adm. fee),* a simple English-style brick cottage offset by boxwood hedges, was built in the 1680s by the grandson of Adam Thoroughgood, who came to the colonies as an indentured servant and became a prosperous landowner.

The drive continues east on I-64 to Va. 44, which rolls right into the heart of 6 **Virginia Beach** *(Visitor Center 757-437-4888 or 800-VA-BEACH).* The state's major ocean

Battle of the Ironclads

Hampton Roads has long been famous as the site of the first Battle of the Ironclads. In early March 1862, the C.S.S. *Virginia,* actually an armored version of the former Federal frigate *Merrimack,* squared off with the North's "cheesebox on a raft"—the *Monitor.* Their four-hour battle ended in a draw. The Monitor sank in a storm off the North Carolina coast later that year, so the two pioneering vessels never dueled again. But their brief encounter introduced ironclad warfare and changed the course of naval history forever.

Tall ship at a harbor festival, Norfolk

resort, this city also happens to be its fastest growing, splaying out in strip malls and housing developments inland from its broad white beach. Beyond the boardwalk and oceanfront high-rises, however, the city hides some compelling surprises. Its far north end sweeps into the curl of **Cape Henry** *(US 60 N, accessible through the Fort Story Army Base Gate),* where not one but two historic lighthouses stand. The **Old Cape Henry Lighthouse** *(757-422-9421. Mid-March–Oct.; adm. fee),* a buff-brick tower offering wide views of the Atlantic, traces its origins to George Washington, who had it built in 1791. Its offspring, the black-and-white checked **New Cape Henry Lighthouse** across the street, has been guiding mariners around the cape since the 1880s. A small monument area beside it recalls the cape's history, and a cross commemorates the spot where, in 1607, Englishmen first landed on what is now Virginia soil. A statue celebrates the heroics of the French naval officer the Comte de Grasse, whose victory over the British in the 1781 Battle of the

Nauticus: The National Maritime Center, Norfolk

Capes eventually led to Cornwallis's defeat at Yorktown.

Another city surprise lies a little south, where the work of early 20th-century mystic and holistic healer Edgar Cayce is perpetuated at the **Association for Research and Enlightenment** *(67th St. and Atlantic Ave. 757-428-3588),* which offers tours and explanations of Cayce's life and abilities.

A little off the beaten path, the **Virginia Marine Science Museum★** *(717 General Booth Blvd. 757-437-4949. Adm. fee)* explores the realms of this state's water world. Overlooking Owls Creek Marsh, the museum consists of two very modern pavilions separated by meadow and woodland. One pavilion explores the life of the marsh itself in whimsical, hands-on, high-tech exhibits. Another pavilion functions as a vast aquarium housing sharks, sea turtles, octopuses, and other animals of the deep. A 3-D, IMAX theater brings their world hurtling out of the screen at you.

From Virginia Beach, head west on Va. 44 and I-264 to downtown 7 **Norfolk.** Bending along the edge of the Elizabeth River, Norfolk is a mix of dilapidated old businesses and shining new waterfront complexes. Chief among these is **Nauticus: The National Maritime Center★** *(1 Waterside Dr. 757-664-1000. Daily May-Sept., Oct.-April Tues.-Sun.; adm. fee),* a battleship-gray behemoth resting atop the city's old Banana Pier. Inside its high-tech three stories, the shipboard experience continues. Virtual reality, live-action adventures, and all kinds of hands-on computers let you enlist your energies in nautical pursuits. On weekends, real—not virtual—ships often berth at the Nauticus dock, opening their gangways to museum visitors. The Navy also maintains its **Hampton Roads Naval Museum** *(757-444-8971)* within the halls of Nauticus, where exhibits tell the tale of area naval affairs.

Norfolk's military tradition has a long lineage. In the Revolutionary War, this important port was held by patriots who refused to succumb to the British. Royal governor Lord Dunmore ordered the town shelled in 1776, and one of his cannonballs still lodges in the brick ribs of **St. Paul's Episcopal Church** *(201 St. Paul's Blvd. 757-627-4353. Tues.-Fri.; donation),* the only building to survive the British burning of the town. The nearby **Willoughby-Baylor House** *(601 E. Freemason St. 757-664-6200. Call for hours; adm. fee),* a stately redbrick town house built in 1794, embodies both Georgian and federal elements. Its tasteful 18th-century furnishings depict the prosperous life of the city during that period. Also an elegant rendering of the same period, the **Moses Myers House** *(331 Bank St. 757-664-6200)* tells the story of the first Jewish family to settle here. Myers, a New York merchant, came from New York in the late 18th century, and his descendants lived here until the mid-20th century. Most of the furnishings are original family pieces.

Virtual reality submarine ride, Nauticus: The National Maritime Center

An incongruous neoclassic temple rises nearby—the domed and columned 1850 city hall designed by Thomas U. Walter, who had a hand in designing the U. S. Capitol. It now enshrines the **MacArthur Memorial** *(Bank St. and City Hall Ave. 757-441-2965. Adm. fee).* Here, controversial general Douglas B. MacArthur is entombed in the mausoleum below the dome, and galleries regale visitors with the general's military prowess.

The superb **Chrysler Museum of Art**★ *(245 W. Olney Rd. 757-664-6200. Tues.-Sun.; donation)* rises in Italianate marble elegance amid the old homes of the city's Hague district. Locals began the museum in 1933 as a low-key art and science collection, but in 1971 it was transformed by the beneficence of Walter Chrysler, Jr., son of the founder of Chrysler Corporation. Now, the museum's cool marble galleries display much of his private collection: world-class artifacts from classical and pre-Columbian to art nouveau and art deco. Also here are the works of Gauguin, Matisse, and a host of other artistic luminaries.

From Norfolk take I-264 and follow signs to 8 **Old Town Portsmouth.** Dozing on the shore of the Elizabeth River, this historic area is replete with well-tended colonial, federal, and Victorian houses. Founded in 1752, the town enjoys an illustrious shipbuilding history; the Confederates used its Gosport Navy Yard to transform the old Federal frigate *Merrimack* into their redoubtable ironclad C.S.S. *Virginia*. The country's first battleship (1892) and first aircraft carrier (1922) were also built here. Such details of the city's shipbuilding past are celebrated at the **Portsmouth Naval Shipyard Museum** *(2 High St. 757-393-8591. Tues.-Sun.; adm. fee).* Permanently berthed nearby, the **Lightship Museum** *(London Slip. 757-393-8741. Adm. fee)* allows a look at life aboard these floating beacons.

Tiffany window, Chrysler Museum of Art

Return to I-264 and follow it west to I-664. The newest bridge-tunnel spanning Hampton Roads, the Monitor-Merrimac, was named for the famous Civil War ironclads that faced off here in March 1862 (see sidebar page 90). Near Newport News, pick up I-64 west, then go south on US 17/J. Clyde Morris Boulevard to the 9 **Virginia Living Museum** *(524 J. Clyde Morris Blvd. 757-595-1900. Adm. fee),* whose birds, reptiles, and other critters are great favorites with kids. The museum also features a boardwalk cantilevered above a marshy pond, with aviaries along the way. A little farther south, on Museum Drive, you'll find the **Mariners' Museum**★ *(100 Museum Dr. 757-596-2222 or 800-581-7245. Adm. fee),* which houses a world-class collection of marine artifacts. Workboats, spiffy little speedboats, a barn full of gondolas, and exotic small craft are on display, as are seascapes in oil, wooden figureheads, and a huge collection of miniature ships. The museum owes its existence to philanthropists Archer and Anna Huntington, who established the original museum in the 1930s. Archer's father, Collis Huntington, founded the Newport News Shipbuilding and Dry Dock Company in the late 1800s, and it remains a vast, roaring concern along the banks of the James.

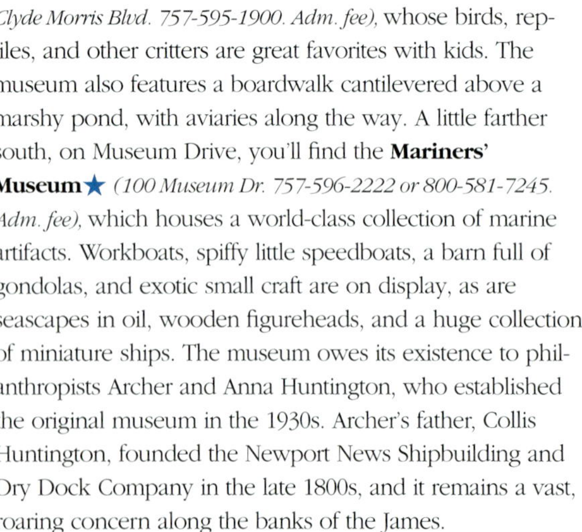

To return to Hampton, backtrack to I-64.

Jefferson Country★★

● **240 miles** ● **2 days** ● **Spring through fall**

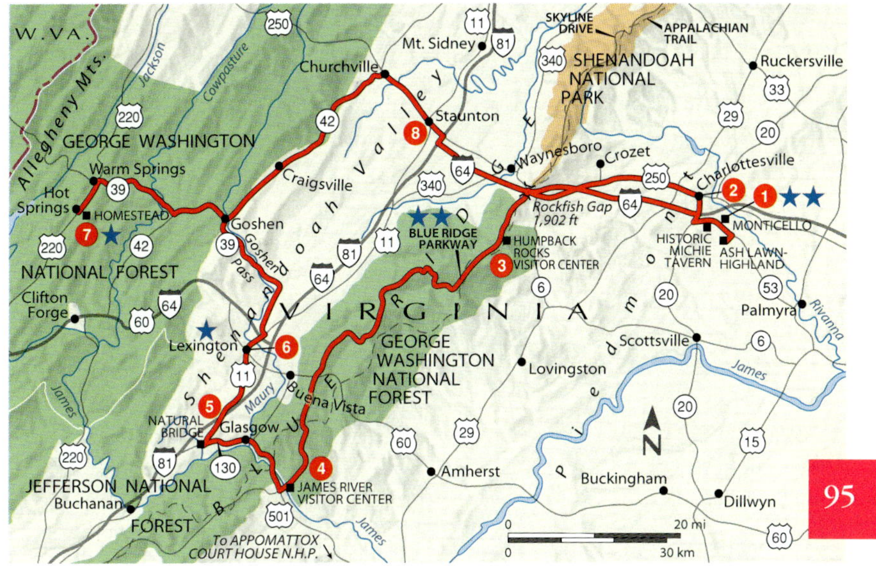

Thomas Jefferson claimed this Piedmont region of Virginia as his personal turf. The drive begins at his famous home, Monticello, then drops down to Charlottesville to visit the University of Virginia, the school he founded. From here the route heads west into the mountains, following the rim-top Blue Ridge Parkway to Natural Bridge. Heading into the Shenandoah Valley, it visits the picturesque college town of Lexington, home to Civil War heroes Robert E. Lee and Stonewall Jackson, before climbing into the Allegheny Mountains. Here, the gracious old Homestead resort—queen of the state's hostelries—still offers spas, golf courses, and southern hospitality. Cascading back down into the Shenandoah, the drive makes a stop in Staunton before returning to Charlottesville.

Thomas Jefferson's Monticello, near Charlottesville

Begin in **Charlottesville,** where the **Monticello Visitor Center** *(Va. 20 S. 804-977-1783)* makes a good starting place for a tour of the area. In addition to regional information, the center offers exhibits detailing Jefferson's private life at his plantation. To see that first hand, follow the signs leading to his nearby Little Mountain— **1** **Monticello★★** *(Va. 53. 804-984-9822. Adm. fee).* The domed residence, recognizable on the face of every nickel, was long in the making; as Jefferson himself admitted, he loved "putting up and tearing down." Its flowing rooms are embued with the tinkering, restless curiosity of a true Renaissance man—from the weighted clock in the entrance hall, to the letter copier he invented, to some of his cherished books. Long windows open onto a roundabout path lined with flowers, and brick dependencies connected to the house hold the workrooms needed to maintain an operating plantation.

"The Corner" near the University of Virginia, Charlottesville

In his later years, Jefferson proclaimed there was "no culture comparable to that of the garden. But though an old man I am but a young gardener." Today his gardens are a focal point at Monticello, and horticulturists diligently cultivate the varieties of fruits, flowers, and vegetables that Jefferson himself grew. Jefferson died here on Independence Day 1826, and his quiet grave on the grounds is marked by an obelisk incised with the epitaph he chose: "Here was buried Thomas Jefferson, Author of the Declaration of American Independence, Of the Statute of Virginia for Religious Freedom, and Father of the University of Virginia."

Just 3 miles south, Jefferson's compatriot James Monroe maintained his own plantation, now called **Ash Lawn-**

Highland *(Off Va. 53 on James Monroe Pkwy. 804-293-9539. Adm. fee).* The simple farmhouse, home to the Monroes from 1799 to 1823, still contains many of their furnishings; a Victorian wing was added by later owners. Today, the plantation sponsors a popular outdoor summer musical series in its boxwood gardens.

Retrace your steps on Va. 53 to **Historic Michie Tavern** *(Va. 53. 804-977-1234. Adm. fee),* below the Monticello turnoff. The 1780s clapboard "ordinary," originally built in nearby Earlysville, features colonial period rooms and colonial-southern cuisine. A 1797 gristmill moved to the grounds exhibits milling procedures of the period.

Turn right at the intersection with Va. 20 into **2 Charlottesville,** where the old downtown has been turned into a successful pedestrian mall. But the town's main focus lies about a mile up Main Street, where sweeping green lawns surround "Mr. Jefferson's University"—the **University of Virginia★★.** Jefferson called the university "the hobby of my old age," and based it "on the illimitable freedom of the human mind to explore...." The historic heart of the university is the neoclassic **Rotunda** *(University at Rugby Rd. 804-924-7969. Guided tours available)* that Jefferson designed in the 1820s, modeling it on Rome's Pantheon. A fire later in the century gutted the interior and for decades the building wore the turn-of-the-century look that architect Stanford White designed for it. A more recent renovation has returned the building to its Jeffersonian majesty, and graceful oval rooms now flow off a central hall. The almost ethereal dome room was once the library.

Behind the rotunda, flanking a shaded green, are the Tuscan colonnades and brick pavilions of Jefferson's academical village. A World Heritage Site, "the Lawn" has also been singled out by the American Institute of Architects as "the proudest achievement of American architecture in the past 200 years." As Jefferson intended, students occupy the small rooms, while the pavilions continue to house senior faculty and some classes. On the outer row of rooms, beyond the gardens, Edgar Allan Poe's room is preserved. The poet spent a year as a student here before his funds ran out, and he enrolled at tuition-free West Point.

From Charlottesville, the drive rolls west on US 250 past the tony horse country of surrounding Albemarle County, where Hollywood celebrities and the scions of

Crozet Pizza

The unlikely small town of Crozet is famous throughout central Virginia for the best pizza in, well, the world. Each perfectly-turned crust and customized mound of fresh veggies, cheese, sausage, and pepperoni is the work of red-haired, red-bearded owner Bob Crum. So loyal are his patrons, ranging from university students to horse country pooh-bahs, that they wear his Crozet Pizza T-shirts all over the world, as evidenced by a bulletin board full of photos of T-shirt-wearing clients atop remote mountains and in the wilds of almost every continent on earth. *(Off US 250, on Va. 240 in Crozet, about 15 miles W of Charlottesville and 10 miles E of entrance to the Blue Ridge Pkwy. 804-823-2132. Tues.-Sat.; reservations advised)*

Blue Ridge Parkway, connecting Shenandoah National Park with the Great Smoky Mountains

American business maintain estates. After climbing up the Blue Ridge to Rockfish Gap, the drive reaches the junction of the north-running Skyline Drive and the **Blue Ridge Parkway★★,** which follows the crest of the southern Appalachians for 469 miles into North Carolina. Head south on the parkway, following the spine of this worn ancient mountain ridge past graceful hardwood forests. At the **3 Humpback Rocks Visitor Center** *(Mile 5.8. 540-943-4716. May-Oct.),* a cluster of log buildings re-create the hard-scrabble life of the old mountaineer farmers in this area. Nearby, a popular hiking trail climbs steadily about a mile to the top of 3,100-foot Humpback Rocks, from whose heights you have a 360-degree view of the pastoral Piedmont countryside and the Shenandoah Valley below.

The drive follows the curvaceous parkway for almost 60 miles to the **4 James River Visitor Center** *(Mile 63.6. 804-299-5496. May-Oct.),* where exhibits and a restored canal lock recall how 19th-century expansionists managed to breach the mountain barrier, building a canal through at this lowest spot to connect western Virginia with the east.

Exit the parkway here and go west on US 501 and Va. 130 to **5 Natural Bridge** *(Va. 130 and US 11. 540-291-2121 or 800-533-1410. Adm. fee).* The Monocan Indians called this 215-foot-high stone archway the "Bridge of God." Thomas Jefferson declared it the "most sublime of nature's works," then proceeded to buy it. Today, a short path leads down to its sylvan setting above Cedar Creek.

From here, follow US 11 north through the **Shenandoah Valley.** Legend maintains that Shenandoah was an Indian word meaning Daughter of the Valley of the Stars. Whether true or not, the poetry still fits this languid, friendly farm country. Settled by German, Scotch-Irish, and American pioneers, it thrived for a hundred years before conflict devastated it. As the breadbasket of the South, it became a much-bloodied battlefield during the Civil War. Several pivotal players in that war had ties to the lovely little valley town of 6 **Lexington**★ *(Visitor Center 540-463-3777).* A simple brick-and-stone town house decorated with Victorian furnishings, the **Stonewall Jackson House** *(8 E. Washington St. 540-463-2552. Adm. fee)* was home to one of the Confederacy's greatest heroes. Thomas Jonathan Jackson lived here blissfully with his second wife before the war, teaching at the Virginia Military Institute, where his eccentric ways earned him the sobriquet "Tom Fool Jackson." Nothing about him—or his house—foretold the legend he would become.

Another monumental southern legend, Robert E. Lee, retired to this quiet town after the war, becoming president of Washington College. Since renamed **Washington and Lee University** *(Letcher Ave. 540-463-8400),* the well-regarded school projects an image of southern gentility in its shaded lawns and columned redbrick buildings. The small Victorian **Lee Chapel** *(540-463-8768),* built under Lee's supervision, houses the famous recumbent statue of Lee by Edward Valentine and the Charles Willson Peale portrait of George Washington, who funded an early precursor to the university. On the lower level lies the small **Lee Museum** and a re-creation of his office. As college president, he explained to his students that "we have but one rule, and that is that every student must be a gentleman." Lee is interred in the chapel's crypt beside his wife, Mary, and their seven children.

Natural Bridge, near Glasgow

The tenor of Letcher Avenue changes abruptly as it enters the grounds of the

Cadets and cannon, Virginia Military Institute

Virginia Military Institute *(540-464-7000),* founded in 1839. Stark military Gothic architecture surrounds the parade grounds, where shoulders-back cadets scurry to class. A place of cherished tradition, the school honors its heroes at the **VMI Museum** *(Letcher Ave. 540-464-7232)* with exhibits tracing the history and development of the school, its faculty, and graduates. In the same building, the **Jackson Memorial Hall** features a mural depicting the charge of the cadets at the Civil War Battle of New Market. A statue of Stonewall Jackson oversees the parade grounds, while the impressive **George Marshall Museum** *(540-463-7103)* stands on the far side, filled with memorabilia to this general and statesman, the impetus behind the post-war Marshall Plan. An extensive library and archives are also housed here.

From Lexington, the drive weaves northwest on US 11 and Va. 39, passing the **Virginia Horse Center** *(540-463-2194),* host to equine events throughout the year. Soon the drive picks up the Maury River, following it through boulder-humped Goshen Pass then up into the Allegheny Mountains. One of the state's finest attractions is located at the small crossroads village of Warm Springs: the **Warm Springs Bathhouses★★** *(Owned by the Homestead. 540-839-1766 or 800-838-1766. April-Oct.; adm. fee),* one for men, one for women. The men's, dating from 1761, is the nation's oldest spa structure and, according to legend, designed by Thomas Jefferson. The women's, built in 1836 along the same lines, was frequented by Robert E. Lee's arthritic wife, Mary, who sought relief in its warm, healing powers. Little changed since Mrs. Lee's day, the natural, stone-lined pools still soothe body and soul with their 98°F mineral waters.

As you leave the bathhouses, turn right onto US 220 south. Four miles down the road you'll spot the massive redbrick tower of the redoubtable 7 **Homestead★** *(540-839-1766 or 800-838-1766)* rising above the small town of Hot Springs. Queen of Virginia's resorts, this 15,000-acre retreat began as a mountain spa in the last century and simply grew from there. Its hallmark redbrick tower

Appomattox Court House N.H.P.

On April 9, 1865, this central Virginia crossroads witnessed the conclusive moment in the Civil War, when Robert E. Lee and Ulysses S. Grant met here and signed terms for the surrender of the Army of Northern Virginia, a surrender that would essentially mean the end of the Confederacy. Many of the buildings, including the courthouse and the Wilmer McLean House where the two generals met, have now been reconstructed, and the National Park Service does a fine job interpreting the last, poignant moments in the fratricidal conflict between North and South. *(Va. 24, about 70 miles SE of Lexington. 804-352-8987. Adm. fee)* looms above a complex of golf courses, riding paths, tennis courts, and the old domed springhouse. During World War II, Japanese diplomats and their families were interned here briefly before being moved to the Homestead's longtime rival, the Greenbrier resort, close by in West Virginia.

Return to Warm Springs and take Va. 39 south through the Allegheny Mountains to the crossroads of Goshen, then follow Va. 42 north and US 250 east into 8 **Staunton** (STAN-ton). A pleasant blend of Shenandoah farmers and college students, Staunton's pleasant old downtown is backdropped by **Mary Baldwin College,** one of Virginia's classic female institutions. Just across from the stark buff buildings of its hillside campus sits the antebellum **Woodrow Wilson Birthplace and Museum** *(18-24 N. Coalter St. 540-885-0897. Adm. fee).* Its columned two-story veranda and decidedly southern character seem slightly out of keeping with the liberal-thinking visionary who went on to become President of Princeton and the nation. In fact, Wilson spent only 11 months here before his father, a Presbyterian minister, was called to a church in Georgia. Still, the museum reflects the kind of childhood that molded the man.

On the outskirts of downtown, the **Museum of American Frontier Culture★** *(1250 Richmond Rd. 540-332-7850. Adm. fee)* does a superb job of tracing the European roots of the Shenandoah Valley. Four working homesteads, three of them brought piece by piece from Europe, show in detail the agricultural and domestic traditions of the German, Scotch-Irish, English, and American families who settled the valley. Costumed interpreters add to the authenticity by explaining to visitors the farming and household chores they're undertaking. To return to Charlottesville, take I-64 east about 40 miles.

Indoor pool, the Homestead resort

Midland Trail

● 275 miles ● 2 days ● Spring through fall

Beginning in the shadow of West Virginia's shimmering capitol dome, this drive moves from urban Charleston into the rural loveliness of southern West Virginia. Following the Midland Trail—US 60—east, it passes the places that make up this state's character: quilting and crafts centers; rivers that rush through narrow gorges and make an industry of white-water rafting; a world-class resort; and an exhibition mine, where you can get a good look at the way thousands of men carved out a living from coal-filled hills and hollows.

Start the tour in ❶ **Charleston** *(Visitor Bureau, 200 Civic Center Dr. 304-733-5469 or 800-344-5075),* rising like an apparition beside the wide brown Kanawha River, its gleaming capitol dome casting a spell across the whole city. This **State Capitol★** *(Greenbrier St. and Kanawha Blvd. 304-558-3809. Guided tours),* considered one of the most impressive in the nation, owes its Renaissance Revival splendor to architect Cass Gilbert, who designed the Supreme Court of the United States as well as the state capitol buildings of Minnesota and Arkansas. Its dome, covered in almost 20 pounds of gold leaf, towers 292 feet. A 4,000-pound Czechoslovakian crystal chandelier hangs from the blue coffered ceiling above the rotunda. Broad marble stairways flank the rotunda, leading to the two legislative wings. Long hallways stretch past more sparkling chandeliers and the low glow of alabaster lamp urns to the impressive senate and house chambers. A statue of Abraham Lincoln, who signed the state into existence, guards the building's south entrance.

On the capitol grounds, the 34-room, Georgian-style **Governor's Mansion** *(304-558-3809 or 800-CALL-WVA. Thurs., Fri. a.m.)* turns its columned face toward the Kanawha River. Designed in 1924 by local architect Walter Martens with the approval of Gilbert, its elegant formal public rooms include a library richly paneled in native butternut.

Next door in the capitol complex rise the contemporary angles of the state's **Cultural Center** *(304-558-0220. Donation)*. Exhibits trace West Virginia history, from pioneering days through steamboating, railroading, and coal mining. The building also displays works by state artists and craftspeople.

Bordering the capitol complex, the streets of Charleston's **East End** *(Self-guided tour maps available from Visitor Center and in capitol rotunda)* are edged by large old Victorian and early 20th-century houses, visible via a paved path along the Kanawha River.

State Capitol, Charleston

Climbing up from the far side of the river, the South Hills are terraced with upscale houses. An old carriage path here twists uphill from the river through the woods to the **Sunrise Museum** *(746 Myrtle Rd. 304-344-8035. Wed.-Sun.; adm. fee)*, occupying two mansions built by the prominent MacCorkle family. The earlier, eclectic Sunrise Mansion (1905), built by former governor William MacCorkle, now houses a hands-on science museum geared to children. From its terrace, views of the city stretch across the river. The **Sunrise Art Museum,** located in the second mansion, built by MacCorkle's son in 1924, features the works of West Virginia artists and others, as well as a program of traveling exhibitions.

The superbly preserved Greek Revival **Craik-Patton House** *(2809 Kanawha Blvd. E., near Daniel Boone Park. 304-925-5341. Mid-April–mid-Oct. Thurs.-Sun.; adm. fee),* dating from 1834, was moved to its present location on the banks of the Kanawha. James Craik, whose grandfather had been George Washington's close friend and personal physician, built his elegantly proportioned columned home in what is now the downtown area. Among the fine 18th- and early 19th-century antiques decorating the house are a number of Craik family pieces. In the mid-19th century, it was owned by Confederate Col. George Patton, grandfather of the World War II hero.

Catawba rhododendron

Head east on US 60 to the neighboring town of **Malden,** which owes its fame to African-American educator and advocate Booker T. Washington. Freed from slavery in the 1860s, the young boy and his family settled in this town, then known as Kanawha Salines. Washington spent his boyhood working in the local salt industry and learning to read and write. A marker on the site of his sister's house *(Malden Dr.)* commemorates Washington, who went on to found the Tuskegee Institute in Alabama. The pink house across the street is home to **Cabin Creek Quilts★** *(4208 Malden Dr. 304-925-9499),* a quilting cooperative that displays and sells the skilled craftsmanship of regional

New River Gorge, Hawks Nest State Park

women. The building itself was constructed in 1838 by the great-grandson of Mary Draper Ingles. Her escape from the Shawnee Indians was made famous in the novel *Follow the River.* Just down the street, in the 1840s **Norton House,** the co-op operates a training and design center displaying museum-quality quilts, including a permanent display of seven patchwork tapestries chronicling 300 years of Malden history. Across the street stands the 1872 **African Zion Baptist Church,** a small white-frame church that ranks as the mother church of the state's African-American Baptists.

From Malden, US 60 follows the wide, deep green Kanawha. In the town of 2 **Cedar Grove,** look for the lovely little roadside **Virginia's Chapel** (1853). Burrowing south through the Kanawha River Valley, the drive reaches the low rumble of the **Kanawha Falls,** overlooked by a pleasant park. A little farther on awaits the riverside **Glen Ferris Inn** *(304-632-1111),* welcoming guests since 1839. The valley broadens out here, to where the Gauley and New Rivers sweep together to form the Kanawha.

The Midland Trail leaves the valley, beginning its climb up onto the Allegheny Plateau and heading toward **Hawks Nest State Park** *(304-658-5196 or 800-CALL-WVA).* A stone-and-log **museum** *(April-Oct.)* here recounts the human and natural history of the area, and a 31-room lodge perches dramatically on the lip of the **New River Gorge★.** From the lodge, a **tram** *(Tues.-Sun. Mem.*

Big Water

This part of West Virginia is famous among rafting aficionados for its "big water." In spring and summer, they flock to the New, a mighty river that rolls through rapids. By early fall, its waters are down and the attention turns to the Upper and Lower Gauley. In September and early October, this boulder-choked little stream becomes a raging torrent, as waters from the Summersville Dam are released into it, transforming it into one of the country's great white-water rivers. The little river can get so clogged with the rafts of commercial outfitters that they have to wait their turns to roller-coaster through the river's Class V rapids. (*For information on commercial outfitters, call 800-VISIT WV.)*

Day–Labor Day and Oct., weekends in Sept.; call for off-season hours; fare) travels down into the gorge, where a concessionaire offers jet-boat tours south up the river, and cliffside trails follow its course north.

The neighboring town of ❸ **Ansted** holds **Contentment** *(US 60. 304-658-5695. June-Aug. Mon.-Sat.; adm. fee),* the restored home of Confederate Col. George Imboden, built in 1830. On the grounds stand a local history museum and a one-room schoolhouse.

A detour off US 60 on US 19 south leads past a multitude of white-water rafting companies operating on the Gauley River and the **New River Gorge National River★.** Four miles down US 19, the river's ❹ **Canyon Rim Visitor**

Rafting the New River Gorge National River

Center *(304-574-2115)* overlooks the stunning gorge and the New River Bridge, the longest single arch steel span bridge in the world. Visitor Center exhibits explain that despite its name the north-flowing New is believed to be one of the oldest rivers on the continent, its origins dating back 65 million years ago to the ancient Teays River. In the recent past, the river gorge became a coal-mining and shipping center, and an abandoned mining camp called Kaymoor One is visible upriver. Its old tipples and mining operation remains are accessible via a hiking trail across the river.

Back on US 60, the drive roller-coasters out of the highlands, through forests frilled with rhododendron and hemlock. Moving into the rolling pastureland of the

Greenbrier Valley, it enters historic little 5 **Lewisburg** *(Visitor Center, 105 Church St. 304-645-1000. Daily Mem. Day–Oct., Mon.-Sat. Nov.–Mem. Day; self-guided walking tour booklet available).* Chartered in 1782, the picturesque town served as a kind of governmental and cultural seat for this region of Virginia, of which it was then a part. A number of late 18th- and early 19th-century buildings still stand, including the limestone **Old Stone Presbyterian Church** *(200 Church St.),* next to the **Lewisburg Cemetery,** dotted with headstones from two centuries.

Reading room, the Greenbrier

On May 23, 1862, the Battle of Lewisburg engulfed this small town. The Union brigade under Col. George Crook (who would later capture Apache Chief Geronimo) bested the Confederate forces of Brig. Gen. Henry Heth, and though the fighting lasted only an hour, some 80 Confederate soldiers died. They are now interred in the **Confederate Cemetery** *(Off McElhenny Dr.),* on a hill overlooking town.

The history of Greenbrier County is reflected in the rich 19th-century furnishings of the **North House Museum** *(301 W. Washington St. 304-645-3398. Mon.-Sat.; adm. fee).* The gracious old house, built in 1820, features a massive sideboard that belonged to Abraham Lincoln's Illinois law partner, John Todd, as well as a series of 1850s prints depicting Virginia spas. The first RFD (Rural Free Delivery) mail buggy in the nation stands on the sunporch, and an adjacent building covers an exceptionally well-preserved 1780 Coffman Conestoga wagon. Across town, the verandaed, antique-filled **General Lewis Inn** *(301 E. Washington St. 304-645-2600 or 800-628-4454)* dates from the early 1800s. The central and west wings, added in this century, were designed by Walter Martens. The inn's, and town's, namesake, Gen. Andrew Lewis, surveyed the area in the 1750s and later fought against the French and the Indians, and eventually the British in the Revolution.

A Greenbrier entrée

Less than 10 miles east of Lewisburg, US 60 enters the town of White Sulphur Springs, whose raison d'être is the renowned 6 **Greenbrier★★** *(304-536-1110 or 800-624-6070).* Situated on 6,500 idyllic acres, the historic, glimmering white resort owes its existence to the sulphur springs located on its grounds and still domed by the Greenbrier's signature springhouse, dating from the 1830s. Rows of white-frame attached cottages originally surrounded the springhouse. One still standing, the two-story **President's Cottage Museum** *(April–late Nov.),* was a preferred vacation spot for five U.S. Presidents in the 19th century. Murals picture the spa's early years and great moments of the Civil War; period memorabilia and photographs of the hotel and its eminent guests capture its traditional élan.

TAMARACK arts and crafts, Beckley

The columned central portion of the current Georgian hotel opened early in the 20th century, and it soon became a watering hole for the country's power brokers. Subsequent decades brought expansion, including a 1960s addition known until recently to only a handful of officials—an extensive bomb shelter, located deep underground, intended to house the U.S. Congress and their families in case of nuclear attack.

Slicing through the Allegheny uplands, head west on I-64 to I-77 north and exit at Harper Road in 7 **Beckley,** hub of this coal-mining region. Signs lead to the **Beckley Exhibition Coal Mine** *(304-256-1747. April-Oct.; adm. fee),* which re-creates an early 20th-century mining camp, with a well-proportioned superintendent's house, a three-room mining-family cottage, a clapboard church, and a museum. But the main draw here is a trip by mine car through the subterranean world of the mine itself. Along the way, former miners-turned-guides do a superb job explaining the dangers of traditional mining and the back-breaking, pick-and-shovel way coal was once wrested from the earth.

Beckley's newest attraction, **TAMARACK: The Best of West Virginia** *(125 Park Ave. 304-256-6843 or 888-TAMARACK)* celebrates the state's strong crafts tradition in textiles, glass, woodworking, and pottery. The capacious modern building holds artist's studios, a cultural center, and a gallery.

The drive returns to Charleston via I-64/77.

Panhandle Loop

● 285 miles ● 2 to 3 days ● Spring through fall

Cook-Hayman Pharmacy Museum, West Virginia University

Diverse and unexpected, this corner of West Virginia shatters stereotypes concerning the state's temperaments and terrains. Beginning in the busy university hub of Morgantown, the drive rambles northwest on backroads that lead through classic hollows and hamlets, where weather-burnished barns advertise chewing tobacco. Picking up the broad trail of the Ohio River, the route heads north to Wheeling, a cosmopolitan community wedged into the narrow finger of the state's northern panhandle. It then moves southeast, following the river through the Ohio Valley, where Native American burial mounds still dot the landscape. In Parkersburg, another major river town with a romantic past, the drive turns east into the hill country settled by 18th-century pioneers who battled the elements and Indians to establish a foothold. Their hardships are still celebrated at re-created forts near Clarksburg, once a glassmaking town and now an oil boomtown.

1 **Morgantown** *(Visitors Bureau 304-292-5081 or 800-458-7373),* home of **West Virginia University** *(Off I-79. 304-293-3489. Guided tours available),* is the starting point for this drive. Established as an agricultural college in 1867, the university now enrolls some 22,000 students in 14 schools and colleges that sprawl across two distinct campuses: the older redbrick campus that sits in the heart of downtown and is the domain of freshmen and sophomores; and the modern Evansdale/Health Sciences campus, scattered along hilltops about a mile away. The two are connected by the university's **Personal Rapid Transit System** *(304-293-5011. Fare),* whose small, amusement-park-style electric cars trundle along their own tracks.

The university's **Core Arboretum** *(Evansdale campus. 304-293-5201)* fills 75 acres of sloping woodland above the Monongahela River. A network of trails weave through a mature floodplain forest, past many of the arboretum's 300 different species of woody plants. Two small museums, open sporadically, are located in academic buildings: The **COMER Museum** *(College of Mineral and Energy Resources Bldg. 304-293-4211)* displays early mining tools and artifacts from the oil and gas industries; and the **Cook-Hayman Pharmacy Museum** *(Health Sciences Center North 304-293-5101)* exhibits an extensive collection of 19th-century pharmaceutical paraphernalia, including tools of the trade, recipes, and jars containing remedies for all forms of ailment.

Barn off US 250, near Cameron

Morgantown is considered the hub of mountaineer country, and, heading west on W. Va. 7, you can see why. Played-out little hamlets wedged into creek hollows no longer thrive from coal mining, but proud signs announce the years that local high schools took the state football championships. Although the general stores are generally closed now and nothing seems to stir, the towns somehow endure amid the beauty of their creek-cloven, wooded world.

At the intersection with US 250, the drive turns north, passing a covered bridge across Rush Run. In about 15 miles, it moves into high, open farm country. At Moundsville, take W. Va. 2 north into **2 Wheeling** *(Visitors Bureau 304-233-7709 or 800-828-3097),* the birthplace of West Virginia. Tumbling up and down bluffs beside the mighty Ohio, the town grew up as a frontier river crossing and continued to grow in the 19th century as a steamboat town, becoming a designated U.S. Port of Entry and the terminus of the National Road (now US 40 and 40A). Its industries—glass, steel, and nails—attracted the German, Irish, and Italian immigrants who gave the town a diverse ethnic flavor.

Capitol Theatre, Wheeling

In 1849 the **Wheeling Suspension Bridge** became the first bridge across the Ohio and the longest cable-hung suspension bridge in the world at that time, spanning 1,010 feet. The 1854 version of the bridge, with its massive antebellum stone towers, still welcomes traffic. Though Wheeling lost its momentum early in this century to the upriver city of Pittsburgh, its riverfront downtown is now slowly reviving. The old federal customhouse, built in 1859, is now **West Virginia Independence Hall** *(1528 Market St. 304-238-1300. Closed Sun. Jan.-Feb.),* with exhibits about the state's role during the Civil War. Between 1861 and 1863, the stately Italian Renaissance Revival building served as the seat of the Restored Government of Virginia. Union loyalists from northwestern counties convened here, rejected Virginia's ordinance of secession, voted to form a new state, and rejoined the Union as the state of West Virginia. Rooms on the second floor re-create the governor's office, and the third floor holds the historic courtroom where the delegates met.

Wheeling Suspension Bridge over the Ohio River, Wheeling

One of the town's old industrial buildings has been renovated to house the **Wheeling Artisan Center** *(1400 Main St. 304-232-1810. Fee for museum)*. A brew pub occupies the first floor; the second, devoted to local history, features **Wymer's General Store Museum,** an authentic re-creation of an 1880s general store. Also upstairs are demonstration areas for artists. Victorian row houses line what is now called **Old Town** at the north edge of downtown. Tours, teas, and dinners in these fine old homes are hosted by the local landmarks foundation *(304-233-1600 or 800-SEE-1870. Tours April-Dec. Wed.-Sun.)*.

Several miles northeast, Wheeling proudly maintains its own resort park—**Oglebay★** *(Off W. Va. 88. 304-243-4000 or 800-624-6988. Adm. fee to attractions)*. Rolling across velvet-green Allegheny foothills, this "city park" ranks as one of the northern panhandle's greatest draws. Conventioneers, golfers, and casual travelers flock to its rusticated lodge and cottages. Hiking paths, a lake, and a zoo dot the complex, but the must-see here remains the Greek Revival mansion that belonged to Earl Oglebay, a Cleveland industrialist and the park's founder and donor. Eight rooms re-create different periods, from a simple frontier kitchen to a high-glossed, Hepplewhite dining room. In the adjacent **Carriage House Glass Museum,** cases gleam with the carnival, cranberry, and pressed glasses for which Wheeling and the Ohio River Valley were famous. The museum's breathtaking 5-foot-high Sweeney Punch Bowl (1844) ranks as one of the largest pieces of cut-glass tableware ever produced.

For a superb view of the river that spawned so much industry, cross into Ohio and follow Ohio 7 south about 10 miles, before crossing back into West Virginia at **3 Moundsville.** In an unassuming neighborhood at the south edge of town, you'll find the reason for the town's name at **Grave Creek Mound State Park** *(Bet. 8th and 10th Sts. 304-843-1410. Adm. fee).* Completed in stages from about 250 to 100 B.C., the large earthwork lying behind the museum was the work of the Adena people who built such burial mounds throughout the Ohio River Valley. This happens to be the largest one surviving, rising almost 70 feet and measuring about 295 feet in diameter. Today vines and bushes cover it, a few trees sprouting up like antlers. A short trail winds up and around to the summit. The park's **Delf Norona Museum** has dioramas and exhibits on the illustrious mound-building culture that held sway over this part of the continent for almost 2,000 years.

Across the street from this sacred place stands an ungodly stone apparition of battlements and crenellations. The now defunct **West Virginia Penitentiary** *(818 Jefferson Ave. 304-843-1993. April-Dec. Tues.-Sun.; adm. fee)* housed criminals from 1866 to 1995. Guided tours recount prison history and lead visitors past preserved jail cells, the gallows, and "old sparky," an electric chair.

Follow W. Va. 2 south for the 70-some-mile stretch to **4 Parkersburg** *(Visitors Bureau 304-428-1130 or 800-752-4982),* where the old downtown and its two adjacent neighborhoods, both national historic districts, have retained their 19th-century charm. Situated at the confluence of the Little Kanawha and Ohio Rivers, the town dates from the 1790s. A decade later, Parkersburg earned its place in history, when Aaron Burr gathered his troops on nearby Blennerhassett Island, hoping to establish his own empire in the Southwest.

Artisan at Fenton Glassworks, Parkersburg

Today, the **Blennerhassett Island Historical State Park★** *(304-420-4800 or 800-CALL-WVA. Stern-wheelers depart from Point Park at 2nd St. Fare. Park open May-Oct.; fee for house tour)* recounts the unfortunate tale of Harman and Margaret Blennerhassett, Irish aristocrats who brought the sophistication of Europe to their island estate in the wilds of the Ohio River Valley. The **Blennerhassett Museum** *(137 Juliana St. April–mid-Dec. Tues.-Sun., mid-Dec.–March Sat.-Sun., and by appt.; adm. fee),* located downtown, houses local history exhibits and includes a film on the family saga. The Blennerhassett mansion, one of the largest houses in America at the turn of the 19th century, sheltered many celebrated guests, including the persuasive Aaron Burr. In 1806 Burr coaxed the couple into allowing him to use their island to quarter his cohorts for his planned conquest of the Southwest. When Burr was arrested for treason, the couple's idyll dissolved and they fled. Though their elegant Italian Palladian home was destroyed by fire five years later, it has recently been reconstructed and once more graces the island. The family so captivated local imagination that many of their furnishings were preserved and have now been returned to the home. The island is accessible via a stern-wheeler that plies the muddy Ohio.

Harman is still said to haunt the historic old **Blennerhassett Hotel** *(320 Market St. 304-422-3131 or 800-262-2536).* Restored to its 1890s gaslight-era grandeur with potted palms, dark wainscot, and marble floors, the turreted red-brick building was once a meeting place of Parkersburg's elite and now enjoys national historic landmark status. At the nearby **Oil & Gas Museum** *(119 3rd St. 304-485-5446 or 304-428-8015. Adm. fee)* exhibits and equipment document

Campsite along the North Fork Hughes River, North Bend State Park

the development of these two industries through the lens of local and national history.

A town gem, **TransAllegheny Books★** *(725 Green St. 304-422-4499. Closed Sun.)*, occupies the imposing neoclassic Carnegie Library that philanthropist Andrew Carnegie gave to the city at the turn of the century. Its stacks, connected by a curving wrought-iron stairwell, are now filled with purchasable used books.

Kitchenware, Pricketts Fort State Park

US 50 knifes due east through the Allegheny foothills here, but it's worth ambling south off the main route for a few miles on W. Va. 31, for a detour to 5 **North Bend State Park** *(Cairo. 304-643-2931)*. Deer browse the park's meadows and woody ridges above the North Fork Hughes River, and trails amble off into quiet hardwood forests. The nearby **North Bend Rail Trail** follows an abandoned railroad spur for 72 miles through the state, part of the coast-to-coast **American Discovery Trail.**

Another short detour off US 50 at West Union leads to the fanciful **Doddridge County Courthouse.** Crowning the highest summit in the hill town, the Romanesque Victorian extravaganza was built, with obvious civic pride, at the turn of the century.

The collection of almost 20 log buildings at **Fort New Salem** *(W. Va. 23. 304-782-5245. April-Dec. Wed.-Sun.; adm. fee)* was moved here to preserve and perpetuate the Appalachian Mountain heritage. The original Fort New Salem was established in the 1790s by Seventh-day Baptist families willing to brave Indians and wilderness to start a new life. Now a part of nearby Salem-Teikyo University, the re-created settlement continues its rich tradition of craft classes and demonstrations, from hearth cooking to weaving, quilting, and candlemaking.

Nearby 6 **Clarksburg,** named for western explorer George Rogers Clark, serves as the urban hub in this part of the state. Continue north on I-79 to return to Morgantown.

Pricketts Fort

At the confluence of Pricketts Creek and the Monongahela River, this stockaded fort is inhabited by costumed interpreters, who retell the hardships faced by early families in this area in the 1770s. Whenever Indian attacks seemed imminent, they would leave their farms and "fort up" here in the cramped quarters, sometimes staying just overnight, sometimes for weeks. In the mid-1800s, the great-grandson of Jacob Prickett built the **Job Prickett House,** which now depicts the simple life of farmers in the area. *(From Clarksburg, head north 20 miles on I-79, then take W. Va. 3 to the fort. 304-363-3030. Mid-April–Oct.; adm. fee)*

Potomac Highland

● 160 miles ● 2 days ● Spring through fall

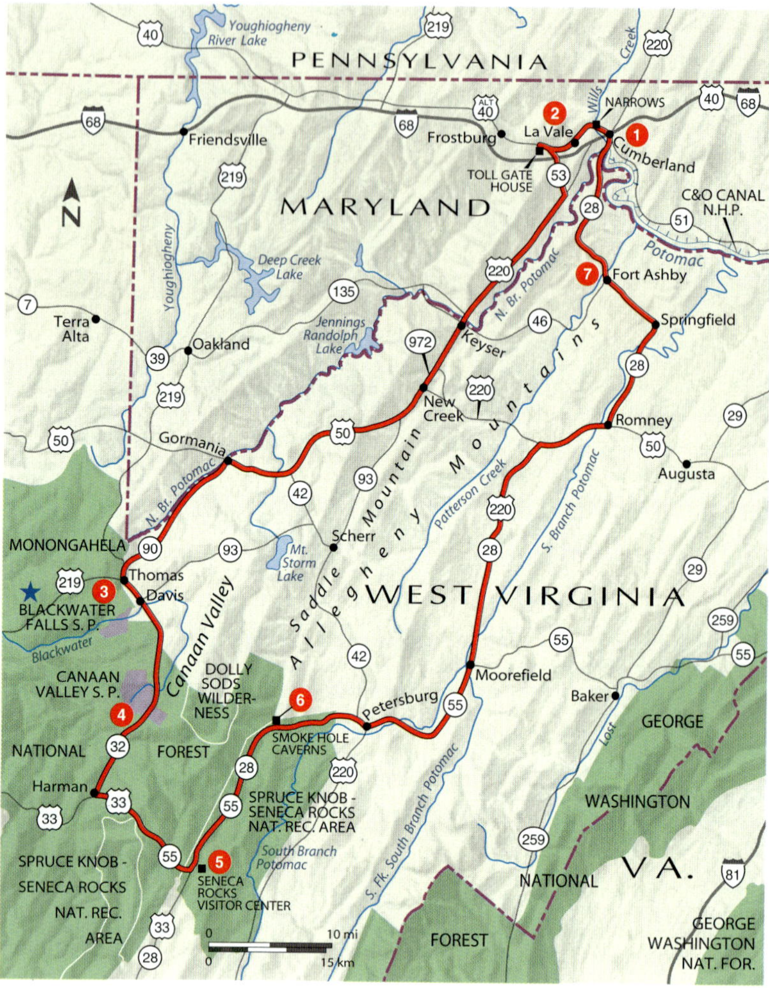

Taking off from the historic, mountain-gap city of Cumberland, Maryland, this drive quickly moves into West Virginia, dipping and turning through the unspoiled Potomac Highland and its spectacular state parks. At Blackwater Falls State Park, ridges and roads overlook one of the loveliest waterfalls this side of the Mississippi. Weaving south, the drive enters the wide-open country of the Canaan Valley before tunneling back into highland terrain and rounding Seneca Rocks, whose high, folded sandstone curves attract climbers and hikers from throughout the East.

Begin in ❶ **Cumberland,** whose warm patina comes from its historic importance as the center of commerce and industry in Maryland's high panhandle country. Situated at a gap in the Allegheny Mountains, the city has been a traditional gateway for goods moving east and west. Its soul was long tied to transportation and industry, and although neither business booms here today, the city celebrates its past.

Cumberland's cavernous old railroad terminal (1913) now houses the **Western Maryland Station Center** *(13 Canal St. 301-777-5905),* a complex that includes a regional

Church spires of Cumberland, Maryland

information center, a small museum with exhibits on glassmaking and railroad memorabilia, and a Visitor Center for the **C&O Canal National Historic Park** *(301-722-8226. Tues.-Sun.).* Cumberland marks the terminus of the 184.5-mile canal that originates in Washington, D.C., and follows the Potomac River northwest. Begun in 1828, the once vital canal is now the domain of bikers and hikers. Remnants of a feeder lock and dam Number 8 still stand just beyond the Visitor Center, but the canal itself here is dry.

Though passenger traffic on the train line to Cumberland was discontinued in 1959, the ***Mountain Thunder*** *(301-759-4400 or 800-TRAIN-50. Daily May-Oct., weekends Nov.–mid-Dec.; fare)* steam train now chugs into the station, taking railroad buffs on a three-hour round-trip excursion through mountain passes to the nearby town of Frostburg.

Settlement in Cumberland began long before the railroad or the canal. In the 1750s, the British established Fort Cumberland to counter threats posed by the French and Indians in the Ohio Valley. An aspiring young colonel arrived here as commander of the Virginia militia, and his small log cabin on Wills Creek, now enshrined as **George Washington's Headquarters** *(Riverside Park at Greene St.),* is all that survives of the original fort. Peer in the window of the small one-room quarters at a mannequined facsimile of Washington looking very military. On the old fort site, the imposing stone **Emmanuel Episcopal Church** *(Washington and Greene Sts.)* has stood since 1851. A walking trail leads past plaques detailing the history of the site.

The church is part of the **Washington Street Historic District,** whose Queen Anne and ornate neoclassic houses are testament to Cumberland's turn-of-the-century affluence. One, the **History House** *(218 Washington St. 301-777-8678. Closed Mon.; adm. fee),* is now owned by the local historical society and furnished in the riotous eclecticism of late Victorian times. Josiah Gordon, president of the C&O Canal, built the Second Empire showcase in 1867.

North Centre Street follows the river west about a mile

Country road, Mineral County, West Virginia

to the **Narrows,** a gap in Wills Mountain made by Wills Creek. A lofty rock pinnacle here soars up 800 feet, long known as Lover's Leap. (The name derives from an apocryphal tale of an Indian princess and her English lover.) Part of the old **National Road,** US 40A, picks up just beyond here on its way through 2 La Vale. After about 4 miles, wedged in among the commercialism, you'll see the small octagonal brick **Toll Gate House** *(301-729-3047 or 301-729-2380. Late May-Oct. Sat.-Sun.).* The first tollhouse on the National Road (1833) and the only one remaining in Maryland, its old rates are still posted on its wall and, even when it's closed, windows allow a look inside at the office and living space of the toll collectors.

Pendleton Overlook at Blackwater Falls State Park, W. Va.

Backtrack to Md. 53 and US 220 south, which leads to the town of Keyser, in Mineral County, West Virginia. South of town, follow US 50 as it climbs Saddle Mountain, then glides down to Gormania. A left turn puts you on W. Va. 90 as it roller-coasters through forests beside the North Branch Potomac River. Small roadside shops cater to tourists heading to 3 **Blackwater Falls State Park★** *(304-259-5216)* and signs point the way. Threaded by the Blackwater River, this memorable parkland takes in an 8-mile-long, boulder-riddled gorge and the high, wooded ridgelines overlooking it. But don't miss the 5-story-high falls that plunge over a limestone ledge and continue their course to the sea. The burnished water that gives the falls and river their names is the result of tannins leached from hemlock and spruce. Most frequented of the park's many trails is the paved one leading down to the falls, whose mists rise heavenward, drenching the evergreens and rhododendrons that hover nearby. Up on the ridge, a pleasant lodge provides spectacular views and reasonably priced meals and rooms. In summer, the park offers horseback riding and swimming and boating on Pendleton Lake. In winter, a Nordic center attracts cross-country skiers.

Fiddlehead ferns, Dolly Sods Wilderness

Spruce Knob-Seneca Rocks National Recreation Area

Return to the little crossroads of Davis and the **Art Company** *(Williams St. 304-259-4218),* a cooperative featuring traditional and contemporary pieces. Continue south on W. Va. 32, rolling into the open spaces of the Canaan Valley, cosetted by the upsweeping Alleghenies, and named, so legend says, by an early European who upon seeing it exclaimed, "Behold, the land of Canaan." Though the valley lies 3,200 feet above sea level, drainage into it from the highland has blessed it with some of the East's most extensive wetlands, which attract all manner of wildlife. A popular resort area, the 4 **Canaan Valley State Park** *(Off W. Va. 32. 304-866-4121)* uses its annual snowfall of 150 to 200 inches to fuel a lively winter ski season. In summer, hikers and golfers flock to the park and its modern, view-filled lodge and scattered cottages. The elevation and temperatures here have produced patches of Canadian-style forests that, owing to their uniqueness at this latitude, have been designated national natural landmarks.

Leaving the state park, W. Va. 32 burrows deep into the vast **Monogahela National Forest** *(304-636-1800),* stretching across more than 900,000 acres. Within the forest lies the 10,215-acre **Dolly Sods Wilderness,** a pilgrimage point for many serious hikers. In this area and the adjacent, lesser-used Roaring Plains, the boulder-strewn terrain, spotted by dwarf evergreens, creates in the wilds of West Virginia a subarctic environment normally confined to Canada.

From Harman, take US 33/W. Va. 55 to the **Spruce Knob-Seneca Rocks National Recreation Area** *(US 33/W. Va. 55. 304-567-2827)*. The weathered Tuscarora sandstone palisades of Seneca Rocks jut 900 feet into the sky. The central gap in the rocks occurred remarkably recently in geologic terms, when an outcropping gave way here in 1987. In the flatland shadow of the rocks sits the 5 **Seneca Rocks Visitor Center** *(W. Va. 28/55. 304-567-2827. Daily April-Oct., weekends Nov.-March)*, and the Sites Homestead, with its 1860s clapboard farmhouse. A 1.3-mile trail toils up the north face of the rocks, but the highland vistas make the climb worthwhile. To continue up the barebone face of the rocks requires technical knowledge and equipment.

Continue north on W. Va. 28/55. Riveting the eastern horizon is another rocky palisade known as Champe Rocks. Soon after, the drive arrives at 6 **Smoke Hole Caverns** *(W. Va. 28/55. 304-257-4442 or 800-828-8478. Adm. fee)*. The same geological activity that formed Seneca Rocks contributed to the creation of this underground landscape, where forces involved in mountain building also produced deep fissures in the surrounding limestone. Water, running through these fissures, eroded and dissolved the limestone, helping produce large passageways and classic formations. The Seneca Indians put the caverns to good use, smoking their wild game in here and giving the caverns their name. Civil War soldiers and moonshiners also made use of the caverns, and the guides giving the tours have a down-home knack of relating tall tales, along with solid explanations of how the caves' flowstone, stalactites, and stalagmites formed millions of years ago.

The drive heads east beside the North Fork South Branch Potomac River through Petersburg Gap, then moseys north through small, friendly towns back to Cumberland. In the town of Ashby, history lovers may wish to visit 7 **Fort Ashby** *(Dan's Run Rd. 304-298-3319. By appt.; donation)*. No more than an oversize log cabin, the fort, recently damaged by fire, is the last of those built in the 1750s by George Washington to fortify the area against Indians.

Mike Smith, owner of Bottling Works Museum, Romney

Civil War Loop★

● 90 miles ● 2 days ● Spring through fall

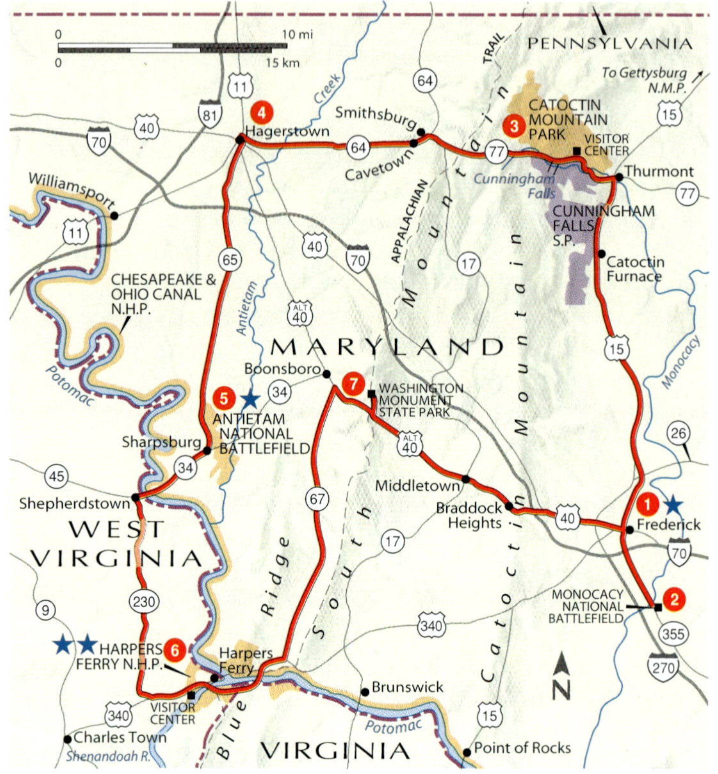

Scarred by war, this foothill wedge where West Virginia and Maryland jigsaw in and out of one another harkens back to its Civil War past. The town of Frederick, starting point for this drive, was trundled through by Union and Confederate troops and made famous by the heroics of a 95-year-old widow. From here, the drive loops north to Thurmont, then west over Catoctin Mountain and on to hardy, German-bred Hagerstown. Here, it heads into serious Civil War country, passing through Antietam, site of the single bloodiest one-day battle in that war, and picturesque Harpers Ferry, where abolitionist John Brown staged a pre-war skirmish.

Start the drive in ❶ **Frederick★,** where, just as in John Greenleaf Whittier's 1860s poem, "The clustered spires of Frederick stand / Green-walled by the hills of Maryland." In the charming old town, well-heeled federal row-houses wall streets laid out in 1745, and walking tours, both guided and self-guided, are offered by the **Visitor Center** *(19 E. Church St. 301-663-8687. Guided tours weekends April-Dec.; fee for tours).* The 1860s county courthouse at **Courthouse Square,** now the city hall, stands with obvious Victorian noblesse, overlooked by other high-toned Victorians and by **All Saints Episcopal Church** *(106 W. Church St.).* A Gothic Revival masterpiece of small, elegant proportions, the 1855 church is ornamented with four stained-glass styles. Francis Scott Key, a Frederick resident and author of "The Star-Spangled Banner," was an active member here. He shared small white-brick **law offices** *(104 N. Court St. Private)* diagonally across the square with his brother-in-law, Roger Brooke Taney, later a Chief Justice of the United States.

At the Barbara Fritchie House and Museum, Frederick

But both share the national limelight with a patriotic little old lady who lived several blocks west. The diminutive brick **Barbara Fritchie House and Museum** *(154 W. Patrick St. 301-698-0630. April-Nov. Thurs.-Mon.; adm. fee)* stands at the edge of Carroll Creek (see sidebar page 125). Fritchie's original home was destroyed by flood and torn down in 1868, but a farsighted niece saved furnishings and building materials, and the current reconstruction incorporates the old floorboards, stairwell, and personal effects.

The stately federal **Roger Brooke Taney House/ Francis Scott Key Museum** *(121 S. Bentz St. 301-663-8687. May-Oct. Sat.-Sun.; adm. fee),* where Taney and his wife lived from 1815 to 1823, saw Key as a frequent visitor. Decorated in period furnishings, the house preserves a desk used by Key and law books of the brothers-in-law. Taney went on to become a controversial Chief Justice of the United States, and his 1857 ruling against former slave Dred Scott was considered a catalyst to the Civil War.

The historic tenor gives way to a lively restaurant and boutique stretch along East Patrick Street. One notable site wedged into this mix is the new **National Museum of**

Civil War Medicine *(48 E. Patrick St. 301-695-1864. Closed Mon.; adm. fee).* Its dioramas and other exhibits recount the still primitive state of medicine during the war.

Drive a few miles south of town on Md. 355 to where the 2 **Monocacy National Battlefield** *(Visitor Center 301-662-3515. Daily Mem. Day–Labor Day, Wed.-Sun. rest of year)* honors the fighting that occurred here along the scenic Monocacy River. In July 1864, Confederate Gen. Jubal Early marched north out of the Shenandoah Valley and along this route, on an invasion course for poorly defended Washington, D.C. The move was designed to divert Union troops away from Lee's forces in Virginia, and the ploy worked. Grant dispatched a corps to intercept Early, and on July 9, the opposing forces tangled in the corn and wheat fields outside Frederick. One of the Northern heroes of the battle, Maj. Gen. Lew Wallace, managed to hold off the Southern troops with his own small band until reinforcements arrived. Today, the battlefield is edged by development and dotted with shrines to the regiments that fought here. The old stone Gambrill Mill now houses the Visitor Center, with an electric map orientation and an interactive computer program on the battle.

Chimney Rock, Catoctin Mountain Park

On the other side of Frederick stands one of the oldest houses in the area, the **Schifferstadt Architectural Museum** *(1110 Rosemont Ave. 301-663-3885. April–mid-Dec. Tues.-Sun.; donation).* The large, plain stone house, built by Joseph Brunner in the 1750s, exemplifies the colonial architecture brought to the area by Germans migrating from Pennsylvania. The unfurnished house is notable for door hinges, hand-hewn oak beams, and other details.

Rose Hill Manor Park *(1611 N. Market St. 301-694-1648. Daily April-Oct., weekends in Nov.; adm. fee)* rises in white Georgian splendor in the countryside just outside town. Geared to children, the manor's gracious rooms and furnishings re-create life in 19th-century northern Maryland. A blacksmith shop, carriage museum, and log cabin are located on the grounds.

From here the drive heads north on US 15 to the small crossroads of **Catoctin Furnace,** where the cavernous stone iron furnace that gave the town its name still presses into a hillside. Established during the Revolutionary War, the furnace continued to produce iron until the beginning of this century.

Follow US 15 briefly to Thurmont, then head west on Md. 77 to the 5,770-acre 3 **Catoctin Mountain Park** *(Visitor Center on Md. 77. 301-663-9343),* where trails wander along streambeds and up mountainsides. The Blue Blazes Whiskey Still Walk, an interesting 0.3-mile amble, leads you to a re-created still on the site of what had been a major moonshine operation in Prohibition days.

About a mile past the park Visitor Center, another short path leads to **Cunningham Falls** *(Cunningham Falls State Park 301-271-7574. Adm. fee),* created as Hunting Creek, a favorite with anglers, rushes down a bedrock ledge. Md. 77 continues through the mountains to the intersection with Md. 64 and on to 4 **Hagerstown** *(Visitor Center 301-791-3246 or 800-228-STAY).* This sturdy town still exudes the hardihood of its early German pioneers, including town founder Jonathan Hager, who arrived here in 1739. His restored stone **Jonathan Hager House and Museum** *(110 Key St. 301-739-8393 April-Dec. Tues.-Sun.)* stands in shaded **City Park,** recalling 18th-century pioneering life. The museum features artifacts found at the site. At the edge of the park's wistful 50-acre lake sits the **Washington County Museum of Fine Arts** *(301-739-5727. Tues.-Sun.; donation),* with a fine collection of 18th- and early 19th-century American art. The city's downtown has a mid-century style to it, save for the **Miller House** *(135 W. Washington St. 301-797-8782. April-Dec. Wed.-Sat.; adm. fee),* an old brick edifice dating from 1818 and now a local history museum.

From Hagerstown, Md. 65 rolls south into the fertile countryside that attracted the early settlers. Its peacefulness belies the turmoil that occurred here on September 17, 1862, when the armies of Robert E. Lee and George McClellan clashed. Now hallowed ground, 5 **Antietam National Battlefield★** *(Md. 65. 301-432-5124. Adm. fee)* enshrines the topography of that conflict. A driving tour passes terrain embedded in the national psyche: tiny Dunker Church, the Cornfield, the Bloody Lane, and others. An observation tower allows an overview of this

Barbara Fritchie

A woman of modest means, Barbara Fritchie was 95 years old when a column of Confederate troops marched by her door. Perhaps mistaking them for Union soldiers or perhaps out of courageous patriotism, Dame Fritchie made her now legendary stance, waving the American flag boldly in their faces. Poet John Greenleaf Whittier heard of her exploit, and, with a poet's love of the romantic, made her into an American heroine for all time. His lines, "'Shoot if you must this old gray head/ But spare your country's flag,' she said," became part of every schoolchild's reciting repertoire. Fritchie's fame carried across the Atlantic, and when Winston Churchill visited the house in the mid-20th century, he recited, after some encouragement, most of the 60-line poem.

124th Pennsylvania Monument, Antietam Natl. Battlefield

place, where some 23,000 men fell in the bloodiest one-day battle in the Civil War. Many Union men are buried in the crossroad of **Sharpsburg,** where row after row of simple white headstones mark the **Antietam National Cemetery.**

Head west on Md. 34, crossing the Potomac River into West Virginia at lovely old **Shepherdstown** *(Visitor Center and walking tour maps, 102 N. King St. 304-876-2786).* Laid out in the 1730s, it ranks as the state's oldest town, its streets still edged by centuries-old houses. So ardent was this town's support of the Revolution that George Washington considered it for the nation's new capital. At the Entler Hotel, established in the 1780s, the **Historic Sheperdstown Museum** *(Princess and German Sts. 304-876-0910. Museum open weekends April-Oct.; donation)* chronicles local history and displays a working copy of an early steamboat.

To the south, ❻ **Harpers Ferry National Historical Park★★** *(Off US 340. 304-535-6298. Shuttle buses from Visitor Center to historic area. Adm. fee)* preserves the historic old town that occupies a rock-riven gorge at the rushing confluence of the Potomac and Shenandoah Rivers. At the end of the 18th century, the area, with its waterpower potential, was chosen as the site of a major federal armory and arsenal. In the 1820s, local inventor John Hall devised a system of interchangeable gun parts, heralding the mass production of weaponry. In 1859 the town's munitions and mountainous location attracted fanatical abolitionist John Brown. On October 16, his 21-man "army of liberation" seized control of the armory. A contingent of Marines under Lt. Col. Robert E. Lee was dispatched to put down Brown's rebellion, and within 36 hours it was over. Brown was later hanged in nearby Charles Town for treason against the state of Virginia.

The Civil War that followed shoved through the town repeatedly, and Harpers Ferry changed hands eight times. In September 1862, Stonewall Jackson's Confederate forces took a record 12,500 Union prisoners here. Today, the town and its rows of brick-and-shale buildings house a variety of Park Service museums. They include the **John**

Gettysburg

About 20 miles north of Thurmont, Maryland, one of the nation's most hallowed sites—**Gettysburg National Military Park** *(Main Visitor Center, Pa. 134. 717-334-1124)*—stretches across the open countryside of southern Pennsylvania. From July 1 to 3, 1863, the worst battle of the Civil War raged here, claiming more than 50,000 casualties. Today, Seminary Ridge, Culp's Hill, Little Round Top, and other scenes of the carnage are preserved in the national battlefield. Self-guided tour brochures and audio tapes *(fee)* are available at the Visitor Center. In the small town of Gettysburg, countless commercial guides offer well-versed tours of the battlefield where so many died and where Lincoln later delivered his history-making address.

Brown Museum, Industry Museum, Wetlands Exhibit, Civil War Museum, African-American Museum, and the **Restoration Museum. John Brown's Fort,** the small brick armory firehouse where Brown barricaded himself, stands near the rivers' confluence. A stone staircase carved into the town's shale hillside leads to the oldest surviving building, the **Harper House,** now interpreted as a tenant apartment like the ones armory workers occupied. Nearby rises the rich stone edifice of historic **St. Peter's Catholic Church.**

On **Virginius Island,** a .75-mile trail *(currently being rebuilt after Jan. 1996 flood damage)* leads past 19th-century industrial ruins. Other trails climb up Maryland and Loudoun Heights to views of the Potomac cutting its water gap through the Blue Ridge, a sight Thomas Jefferson proclaimed "perhaps one of the most stupendous scenes in Nature."

Continue on US 340, turning north on Md. 67 to US 40A. This route weaves up and around the bends of South Mountain to **Washington Monument State Park** *(301-791-4767).* A short, wooded path leads to the top of the mountain and a stone monument, the first ever erected for the "Father of the Country." It was built by volunteers from nearby Boonsboro in 1827 and used during the Civil War as a Union signal station. Expansive views of the fertile Maryland countryside spread below into the distance.

To return to Frederick, the starting point of this drive, continue east on US 40A and US 40.

Harpers Ferry and the Shenandoah and Potomac Rivers from the cliffs of Maryland Heights

Baltimore to Annapolis★

● 50 miles ● 2 to 3 days ● Year-round

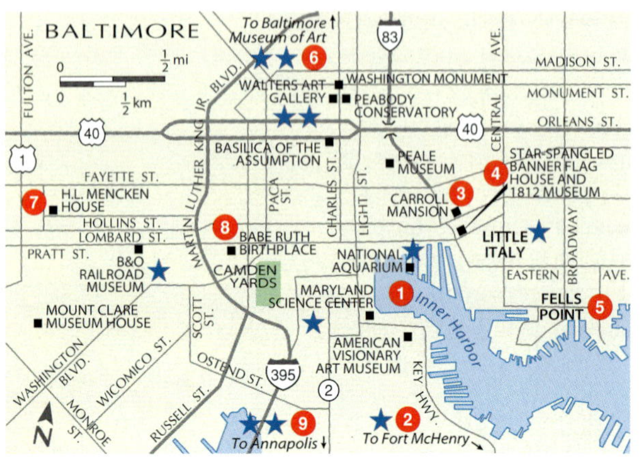

The spirited old port city of Baltimore is the starting point for this drive. Filled with museums, boisterous neighborhoods, and long-lasting traditions, "Bawlamer" makes its own distinct contribution to the American landscape. From there the drive rolls south on Md. 2 through suburbs and horse country to the historic state capital of Annapolis. Home of the U.S. Naval Academy and a major yachting center, Annapolis hugs the mouth of the Severn River as it empties into the Chesapeake Bay.

Begin in **Baltimore★★** *(Visitor Center, 301 E. Pratt St. 410-837-4636 or 800-282-6632).* Fun-loving, culture-filled, energetic, and proudly ethnic, "Charm City" could charm anyone. The once run-down waterfront of this old port on the banks of the Patapsco became one of the country's first festival parks in the 1970s, and the ❶ **Inner Harbor** area now ranks among the most popular tourist stops on the East Coast. Centered around the piers where seafood and produce boats once berthed, the area features museums, summer musicians, food and boutique pavilions, and the same neighborliness that infuses the rest of the city.

The signature attraction here has long been the **National Aquarium★** *(501 E. Pratt St. 410-576-3800. Adm. fee).* Its glass "prows" and whimsical angles lean into the Inner Harbor from the end of Pier 3. At its entrance, seals frolic in an outdoor pool, while inside some 9,000 aquatic creatures circle around huge pools and smaller aquarium tanks. The aquarium

Visitors to the National Aquarium

holds the largest collection of stingrays in the country as well as the Marine Mammal Pavilion, where bottlenose dolphins disport in an amphitheater filled with enthusiastic audiences. In the unforgettable 225,000-gallon open-ocean tank, sharks and other unblinking denizens circle endlessly. Other major exhibit areas explore specific

Baltimore skyline at night

ecosystems—an Atlantic coral reef, graced by hundreds of brilliantly colored tropical fish; an undersea kelp forest; a humid, lush South American rain forest; and Maryland's water cycle from the mountains to the sea.

Also on Pier 3, the **Baltimore Maritime Museum** *(410-396-3453. Adm. fee)* comprises three pierside vessels. The U.S.S. *Torsk,* a World War II-vintage submarine that made almost 12,000 dives in its career; the U.S. Coast Guard cutter *Roger B. Taney,* survivor of Pearl Harbor and Japanese kamikaze attacks; and the old lightship *Chesapeake,* which served as a floating beacon and research vessel for decades.

On the far side of the Inner Harbor another stellar museum, the **Maryland Science Center**★ *(601 Light St. 410-685-5225. Adm. fee),* offers the curious of all ages an opportunity to explore many kinds of scientific concepts in three floors of hands-on, state-of-the-art exhibits. A planetarium and IMAX theater enhance the experience.

The Inner Harbor's latest museum showcases the growing appreciation for "outsider" or "naive" art. The **American Visionary Art Museum** *(800 Key Hwy. 410-244-1900. Mem. Day–Labor Day Tues.-Sun., rest of year Wed.-Sun.; adm. fee)* highlights carvings, paintings, dioramas, and other intuitive masterpieces by America's self-taught artists. The contemporary museum building actually incorporates two old harbor warehouses, the Baltimore Copper Paint Company and the Four Roses whiskey warehouse.

Federal Hill shoulders against the rear of the museum, edged by buttoned-down 19th-century row houses. Its grassy park affords a superb view of the Patapsco as it sweeps into the Inner Harbor—a vantage not lost on military men, who used this hill as a lookout in both the War of 1812 and the Civil War. Today, a statue of Maj. Gen. Samuel Smith, a hero of the War of 1812, looks out onto the burgeoning Baltimore cityscape.

At downtown's southern edge, 2 **Fort McHenry National Monument and Historic Shrine**★ *(End of E. Fort Ave. 410-962-4290. Adm. fee)* still guards the Patapsco River as it funnels into Baltimore. Now administered by the National Park Service, the star-shaped fortress encircles brick barracks, guardhouses, and gun batteries. Built in the 1790s, it became key to Baltimore's defense when the British attacked the city in September 1814. The Colonials repulsed the British in a night battle that raged along the waterfront. In the morning, the victorious Americans hoisted the enormous flag made by Mary Pickersgill, tooting the British out of the harbor to the sound of "Yankee Doodle."

Downriver from the battle, an influential Washington lawyer watched the procedures from a U.S. truce ship. Francis Scott Key had been in the area since early

"Little Dancer, 14 Years" by Edgar Degas, Baltimore Museum of Art

September, negotiating with the British for the release of a friend, Dr. William Beanes. On September 14, "by the dawn's early light," he saw the star-spangled banner waving above Fort McHenry and was inspired to pen what would become the national anthem.

Encompassing a variety of historic sites the **Baltimore City Life Museums★** celebrate the city's vibrant cultural diversity: The **Peale Museum** *(225 Holliday St. 410-396-1149. Sat.-Sun.; adm. fee)*—built in 1814 by artist Rembrandt Peale, son of portraitist Charles Willson Peale—was intended as an "elegant rendezvous for taste, curiosity, and leisure." The Peales pioneered the concept of museums in America and this is the oldest museum building in the country. Today it holds three floors of works by the Peale family and the kinds of scientific curios displayed in 19th-century museums.

Other Baltimore City Life Museums cluster a few blocks away at the east edge of downtown, around the old ❸ **Carroll Mansion** *(33 S. Front St. 410-396-3523. Adm. fee).* Charles Carroll, a prominent statesman and signer of the Declaration of Independence, spent his last winters in this early 19th-century house, and its current empire furnishings reflect the family's prestige and lifestyle. The far simpler life of a middle-class wheelwright's family is re-created at the adjacent **1840 House.** The complex also includes the **Center for Urban Archaeology,** which, despite its name, offers an innovative and lively look at what gives the city its distinctive character. Although a new structure, the building wears an impressive cast-iron facade, salvaged from an old fruit-company warehouse.

A block north, the landmark redbrick **Shot Tower** *(801 E. Fayette St. 410-396-3523)* rises 215 feet. Threatened by urban renewal and demolition earlier in this century, this rare piece of Americana was saved from the wrecking ball by preservationists. Built in 1828, it, like other such towers of the time, was an ingenious device for creating lead shot. From its heights, molten lead was dropped down a shaft, forming into the desired ball-shaped ammunition during the descent.

Retrace your steps a couple blocks down Albemarle Street to the ❹ **Star-Spangled Banner Flag House and 1812 Museum** *(844 E. Pratt St. 410-837-1793. Tues.-Sat.; adm. fee).* This modest, pleasant house recalls one of Baltimore's finest moments. With an imminent threat from the British hanging over the city during the War of 1812, officials sought out the home's owner at that time, local flagmaker Mary Pickersgill, and commissioned her to make an enormous version of the Stars and Stripes to wave above Fort McHenry. The resulting 30-foot by 42-foot version of the star-spangled banner inspired Francis Scott Key to write the national anthem. Mary's flag now hangs in the Smithsonian's Museum of American History, but a video and small museum here recount Baltimore's involvement in the war, and the rest of the house re-creates the period of her tenure.

From here, the narrow streets of **Little Italy★** twist past family-run restaurants, bakeries, mom-and-pop stores, and the small, neat form-stone row houses that characterize this part of the city. Generations of Italian-American families have lived, worked, worshiped, and celebrated their ethnic identity here. Long a city of ethnic neighborhoods, old Baltimore still claims Polish, Greek, African-American, and other enclaves. Wedged among them and adjacent to Little Italy is the now trendy historic district of 5 **Fells Point** *(Foot of Broadway),* where the city originated in the early 1700s. Old brick row houses from the era when this was a busy colonial shipbuilding site have been restored, and shops and cafés line Brown's Wharf and Thames Street.

Baltimore also holds a number of acclaimed cultural institutions. The **Walters Art Gallery★★** *(N. Charles and Centre Sts. 410-547-9000. Tues.-Sun.; adm. fee),* north of downtown, contains one of the finest private collections in the country. Self-made railroad and investment tycoon William T. Walters began collecting in the mid-1800s, displaying his art in his home on fashionable Mount Vernon Place. His son Henry picked up where his father left off and today their extensive collection, spanning 5,000 years, fills three adjacent buildings, including the vast Italian Renaissance palazzo that Walters built. Greek, Roman, Egyptian, Ethiopian, and Etruscan statuary and jewelry are found here, including the renowned Ruben's Vase (A.D. 400). Carved in Constantinople from a single agate, it is widely recognized as a rare masterpiece of antiquity. Other galleries are devoted to the paintings of such Old Masters as Raphael, Tiepolo, and El Greco, and to 19th-century innovators like Monet, Pissarro, and Corot. The rich collection of decorative arts includes Sévres porcelains and works by Tiffany and Fabergé. The museum's newly renovated Gothic Revival Hackerman House (1850) is devoted to art

The Preakness at Pimlico

The Preakness, the second event in horse racing's Triple Crown, got its start here on the northwestern outskirts of Baltimore in 1873. The Maryland Jockey Club, founder and still owner of the course, was organized years before in Annapolis, a big horse racing center in colonial times. Such prominent Marylanders as William Paca and Charles Carroll were early members of the club, as was President Andrew Jackson. Held the third Saturday in May, the race for three-year-olds attracts thousands of spectators and the attention of racing enthusiasts worldwide. *(Pimlico Race Course, Hayward and Winner Aves. 410-542-9400)*

Camden Yards, home of the Baltimore Orioles

from Japan, China, India, and Southeast Asia.

Mount Vernon Place Park is anchored by the 1829 **Washington Monument** *(Monument and Charles Sts.)*. Predating the one in the nation's capital, it was designed by the same architect—Robert Mills—who topped this Doric shaft with a statue of the first President. Across the street from the monument, the respected **Peabody Conservatory of Music and Library** occupies another impressively ornate Renaissance Revival building. A few blocks west, the **Maryland Historical Society** *(201 W. Monument St. 410-685-3750. Tues.-Sun.; adm. fee)* recounts the history of the state in a succession of galleries that extend through several buildings, including the 1840s mansion built by industrialist and philanthropist Enoch Pratt, best known as the founder of the **Enoch Pratt Free Library** *(400 Cathedral St.)*.

The neighborhood also claims the stately **Basilica of the National Shrine of the Assumption of the Blessed Virgin Mary** *(Cathedral and Mulberry Sts. 410-727-3564)*, the nation's first Roman Catholic cathedral and mother church of U.S. Catholicism. Renowned early 19th-century Washington architect Benjamin Latrobe originally designed the massive domed and columned Greek Revival structure (the twin towers were later additions). It opened its doors in 1821.

Along the northern edge of town, on the shaded campus of distinguished Johns Hopkins University, stands another stellar city institution, the 6 **Baltimore Museum**

of Art ★★ *(Art Museum Dr. 410-396-7100. Wed.-Sun.; adm. fee).* The state's largest art museum, its collection ranges from the ancient through the contemporary. The original marble classical revival building, designed in the late 1920s by John Russell Pope, now houses superb American decorative arts; European Old Masters; the tribal art of Africa, America, and Oceania; and Asian ceramics. But the premier

Annapolis Harbor

attraction here is the Cone Collection, among the most outstanding collections of 19th- and 20th-century art in the world. The Matisses, Picassos, Renoirs, Cézannes, and van Goghs featured here were purchased by the Cone sisters—Dr. Claribel and Miss Etta Cone. Wealthy Baltimore natives and friends of American expatriate writer Gertrude Stein, the sisters traveled abroad annually, often visiting Stein in Paris, and through her coming into contact with the Parisian art world of the early 20th century. At Etta's death in 1949, the preeminent collection was left to the Baltimore Museum. One gallery room now re-creates the Cone parlor, hung with Postimpressionist masterpieces.

The museum's West Wing for Modern Art features large canvases of mid- to late 20th-century works by such notables as Andy Warhol and Mark Rothko. Two sculpture gardens, located on the east side of the museum, highlight both small and monumental pieces and include works by Auguste Rodin, Alexander Calder, and Louise Nevelson.

Southwest of downtown, the 7 **H. L. Mencken House** *(1524 Hollins St. 410-396-7997. Sat.-Sun. or by appt.; adm. fee),* a City Life Museum, occupies the substantial row house overlooking Union Square where the American journalist, called the Sage of Baltimore, lived and worked. Many of his belongings are still in place. The nearby **B&O Railroad Museum★** *(901 W. Pratt St. 410-752-2490. Adm. fee)* radiates out from an 1884 roundhouse that shelters vintage steam, diesel, and electric locomotives. Outside, the old yards are filled with one of the most impressive collections of rolling stock on the continent. The museum entrance is housed in the 1830s Mount Clare Station, the nation's first railroad station. In Carroll Park is the **Mount Clare Museum House** *(1500 Washington Blvd. 410-837-3262. Closed Mon.; adm. fee),* the only pre-Revolutionary structure still standing in the city. Charles Carroll, who authored the Maryland Declaration of Independence, built the Georgian house in 1754, and it still contains many original furnishings.

Back toward downtown, baseball honors its largest legend at the 8 **Babe Ruth Birthplace and Baseball Center** *(216 Emory St. 410-727-1539. Adm. fee).* This modest row house displays photos, live-action footage, and other Ruth memorabilia. Though Ruth played for the Red Sox and the Yankees, the house also commemorates great moments in the Baltimore Orioles' history.

The "O's" new home occupies nearby **Camden Yards** *(333 W. Camden St. 410-547-6234. Call for tour times; fee for tours),* where the mid-1800s buildings of this former B&O rail yard have been incorporated into a stunning state-of-the-art ballpark. In 1995 the Orioles' Cal Ripken, Jr., entered baseball history when he broke the Major League Baseball record (2,130) for the number of consecutive games played. Buy tickets early if you're interested in attending a game.

The drive now leaves Baltimore, following Hanover Street (Md. 2) south past the suburban enclaves of Glen Burnie and Severna Park. Picking up the Severn River, the route parallels the river into 9 **Annapolis★★** *(Visitors Bureau, 26 West St. 410-280-0445).* In 1694 this site at the confluence of the Severn and the Chesapeake Bay was ordained Maryland's new capital by royal governor Francis Nicholson, who laid out the web of narrow streets that still gives the city much of its considerable charm.

Then, as now, the streets of the historic district radiate

Middies vs. Johnnies

Cherished rivals, the intellectual "johnnies" of St. John's College and the robust "middies" of the U.S. Naval Academy have developed a courtly means of sparring. Every April, under St. John's sprawling 400-year-old Liberty Tree, they square off in a rousing croquet match while crowds of onlookers, sporting wide-brimmed hats and the flowing clothes of yesteryear, join in the fun.

out from the **State House** *(State Cir. 410-974-3400),* the oldest state capitol in continuous use in the country. In 1780 the legislature first convened here and has done so ever since. The fledgling U.S. Congress also met here briefly in the early 1780s and during that time ratified the Treaty of Paris, ending the Revolution. George Washington appeared before that Congress to resign his commission as commander in chief of the Continental forces. A Charles Willson Peale painting hanging in the State House depicts Washington at the Battle of Yorktown.

Long before that battle was fought, Annapolis had become Maryland's most prosperous port and one of the country's most cosmopolitan cities. During the Revolutionary War confident Annapolitans threw their support firmly behind the colonial effort. One of them, Mathias Hammond, even undertook to build an elaborate town house in the midst of the war. The gracious Georgian **Hammond-Harwood House** *(19 Maryland Ave. 410-269-1714. Adm. fee),* with its lovely proportions and woodwork, was the creation of William Buckland, who had previously worked on George Mason's Gunston Hall, in Virginia. (Buckland had arrived in Virginia as an indentured servant and prospered through his considerable talent.) Ironically, one of Buckland's descendants, William Harwood, became a proprietor of this Annapolis house, and many Harwood family pieces now decorate it, along with Charles Willson Peale portraits.

Buckland also worked on the **Chase-Lloyd House** *(22 Maryland Ave. 410-263-2723. Tues.-Sat.; adm. fee),* across the street. Samuel Chase, who had the house built in the 1770s, would later become a Supreme Court justice. But the grandest house in town was and is unquestionably the **William Paca House and Garden★★** *(186 Prince George St. 410-263-5553. Limited hours Jan.-Feb.; adm. fee).* Palatial in its size and elegance, the house was built in 1765 by a signer of the Declaration of Independence and a governor of the state, William Paca. Two acres of gardens cascade down behind the manor in formal parterres and terraces.

A couple of blocks north, Prince George Street intersects College Avenue, from whose edge rises the small but genteel campus of **St. John's College** *(College Ave. bet. St. John's and King George Sts. 410-263-2371).* The college is renowned for its distinctive great books curriculum—covering only classic works of literature, science, and

How to Crack a Crab

If you're not a fussy soul, the crab houses that dot Chesapeake Bay towns are the liveliest and most enjoyable way to feast on the bay's "beautiful swimmers"—the succulent blue crabs. Your waitress or waiter will dump a dozen spicy steamed crabs on the brown-paper tablecloth in front of you, and you can dig in. Mallets for crushing and hands for picking are the appropriate cutlery in this setting, and your server will probably be happy to show you the easiest way to get at the meat of these crustaceans, which really isn't hard. Debates swirl as to what condiments go best with crab. Some like melted butter and others prefer hot sauce. Try both and decide for yourself.

philosophy—and for its sprawling 400-year-old Liberty Tree. Under its branches the city's 18th-century patriots met to swear allegiance to the Revolutionary cause.

The city's other—and far larger—institute of higher learning is the **U.S. Naval Academy**★ *(Visitor Center adjacent to Halsey Fieldhouse at Randall and King George Sts. 410-263-6933. Guided tours available).* Encompassing 300 acres along the riverfront, the academy has maintained its traditions at the gracious, tree-lined "Yard" since 1845. Square-shouldered mid-shipmen—"middies"—bustle around the Yard's impressive, green-roofed beaux arts buildings, many designed at the turn of the century by Ernest Flagg. In the academy's landmark, domed chapel, sunlight filters in through Tiffany stained-glass windows. In the chapel's lower-level crypt, the marble sarcophagus of Revolutionary War hero John Paul Jones is ringed by ceremonial flags and accoutrements and guarded by square-jawed marines.

Chesapeake Bay feast of spicy steamed crabs

The busy heart of Annapolis lies on the waterfront around Market Square. The small 1858 **Market House** still occupies its center, now filled with food shops. Nautical motifs and stores abound, and out on the river the blossoming sails of private sloops vie for room to maneuver. Sailing hub of the Chesapeake Bay, Annapolis is hallowed ground for yachtsmen, and the City Dock area in front of Market Square has, for obvious reasons, been dubbed "Ego Alley." But the city also caters to nonsailors. Good restaurants are plentiful, with fine local seafood and live music almost every day of the week; lots of shops and boutiques carry merchandise that has nothing at all to do with sailing.

To return to Baltimore, you can take US 50 west to I-97 north or retrace your steps along Md. 2.

Eastern Shore★

● 230 miles ● 3 days ● Spring through fall

From the legendary Brandywine Valley estates of the du Pont barons, this drive curves south to New Castle, whose quiet shaded streets reflect its Dutch and British colonial heritage. Winding through blankets of green farm fields, the drive explores the rural Eastern Shore, stopping at a Civil War fort and the historic 18th-century village of Odessa before heading into the rich marshlands along the Delaware River. At Dover, Delaware's capital, a variety of museums explore the First State's heritage, and a nearby wildlife refuge allows a close look at migratory birdlife.

Passing through small towns and into Maryland, the drive visits the cities of Easton and St. Michaels, where the gentry and the watermen of the Eastern Shore are celebrated. Looping north back to Wilmington, the drive passes through Chestertown, whose elegant houses slumber on the Chester River, and the old canal town of Chesapeake City.

The drive begins at perhaps the state's most remarkable attraction—1 **Winterthur Museum, Garden and Library**★★ *(Del. 52, 6 miles N of Wilmington. 302-888-4600 or 800-448-3883. Adm. fee).* Over the course of his lifetime, scion Henry Francis du Pont turned his family estate into the country's most extravagant celebration of the American decorative arts. The house, nested in the lush green hills of the Brandywine Valley, originated in 1838 with a Greek Revival mansion built by du Pont relatives. Henry's father added a modest addition, but when Henry inherited it in the late 1920s, he doubled its size and at about the same time became interested in the American decorative arts. For the rest of his life he collected avidly, and in 1959 he added an immense seven-story addition to his home to display his collections for public exhibit.

Today, du Pont's legacy enjoys worldwide renown, with 175 period rooms and close to 90,000 artifacts capturing every style and tradition in American decorative arts, concentrating on the era of handcrafting from the 17th century to the dawning of the industrial age.

Winterthur Museum, just north of Wilmington

Entire rooms, from the paneling, wainscot, ceiling molding, flooring, and fireplace "surrounds," have been dismantled and re-created at Winterthur. The best of American china, cabinetry, portraiture, and silver are preserved and explained in a variety of tours that cover different aspects and areas of the estate. A new gallery addition is devoted to changing exhibits examining in detail various aspects of the decorative arts. Surrounded by almost 1,000 acres of rolling piedmont, the estate is graced by a naturalistic garden of azaleas, wildflowers, peonies, and woodlands, including a pinetum where evergreens from worldwide reach skyward. Trained at Harvard as a horticulturist, du Pont was a devout gardener, and chose his daily china to match whatever flowers had been cut to ornament the table.

One of Henry's descendants, John du Pont, inherited his love of the natural, and helped establish the **Delaware Museum of Natural History** *(Del. 52 just S of Winterthur entrance. 302-658-9111. Adm. fee),* where dioramas, exhibits, and public programs highlight the museum's main collections of shells, birds, and mammals. From here, head south on Del. 52, then east on Del. 141 to the **Hagley Museum and Library**★★ *(302-658-2400. Call for hours; adm. fee).* At the beginning of the 19th century, Éleuthère Irénée du Pont arrived here from France and recognized this spot on the banks of the Brandywine as well suited to his entrepreneurial intentions. He forthwith established the black-powder mill that would give rise to the gigantic DuPont Company. Hagley, as the site was called, became the largest manufacturer of black powder in the world, stretching for 2 miles along the Brandywine and in constant use until 1921. Many of the granite buildings still stand as picturesque ruins along the now forested riverbank. Telling the tale of American industrialism, the 230-acre museum site interprets life here at the industrial plants and workers' village. The original du Pont estate, Eleutherian Mills, is included on the tour, with period rooms and furnishings recapturing the life of the last du Pont heiress to live here.

Stairway and fountain, Nemours Mansion and Gardens

Proceeding east on Del. 141, follow the signs to **Nemours Mansion and Gardens★** *(1600 Rockland Rd. 302-651-6912. May-Nov. Tues.-Sun.; adm. fee).* The lavish 102-room French château of Alfred I. du Pont was designed by Carrère and Hastings of New York in the early 1900s. Like some mini-version of Versailles, it unabashedly boasts room after room of antiques, paintings, rugs, and tapestries. The 300 acres surrounding it are landscaped with formal gardens, riotous fountains, statuary, and staircases that seem to indicate an unrestrained taste for the luxurious. However, this du Pont shared the family penchant for philanthropy and established a children's medical facility on the estate.

Immanuel Episcopal Church, New Castle

The du Ponts were not the only moneyed clan to build palatial complexes in the countryside around Wilmington, and a different take on the high life is available farther east via Del. 141 and Wilson Street at **Rockwood Museum★** *(610 Shipley Rd. 302-761-4340. March-Dec. Tues.-Sun., Jan.-Feb. Tues.-Sat.; adm. fee).* Native Delawarean Joseph Shipley, great grandson of Wilmington's founder, William Shipley, made his fortune in England and returned to this area in 1851. Influenced by his years abroad, he built a British-style country house, with gables, light-filled rooms, and a typical central stairway. The house now reflects the furnishings and lifestyle of Shipley's turn-of-the-century descendants, with added touches of Irish country-manor living. The grounds retain the rounded shrubs and contrasting evergreens popular in the mid-19th century.

Ensconced in an upscale, 20th-century Wilmington neighborhood lies the **Delaware Art Museum** *(2301 Kentmere Pkwy. 302-571-9590. Closed Mon.; adm. fee).* Inside the modern brick building is a renowned collection of English, Pre-Raphaelite paintings, with works by Dante Gabriel Rossetti and others. The American galleries include works by the Wyeths (who live in the Brandywine Valley), Winslow Homer, Thomas Eakins, John Sloan, and Claes Oldenburg.

Take I-95 and Del. 141 south through Wilmington's commercial suburbs to ❷ **New Castle★★.** Village-size by

Sunrise over the Delaware River from Del. 9, near Wilmington

modern standards, this peaceful spot on the banks of the upper Delaware River has witnessed a lot of history. The Dutch arrived here in 1651 and established Fort Casimir. Three years later, the Swedes took it for a year before Peter Stuyvesant grabbed it back, making it the Dutch capital of the Delaware region. By 1664 the British had bested the Dutch and given their holdings to William Penn, who first set foot on American soil at the end of what is now Delaware Street. He gave the town its name, and the city thrived as the colonial capital until the Revolution.

Seemingly little changed since then, the town is a well-preserved jewel of 18th- and 19th-century town houses centered around a village green. Although the original Dutch legacy is little evidenced, you can find a quaint vestige of it at the small, low-ceilinged **Dutch House** *(32 E. 3rd St. 302-322-2794. March-Dec. Tues.-Sun., Jan.-Feb. weekends only; adm. fee),* built about 1700 and furnished with period pieces. The 1738 Georgian **Amstel House** *(4th and Delaware Sts. 302-322-2794. March-Dec. Tues.-Sun., Jan.-Feb. weekends only; adm. fee)* re-creates the life of a prominent 18th-century New Castle family. On the town green, the 1703 **Immanuel Episcopal Church,** gutted by fire in 1980, has been beautifully restored, and its cemetery memorializes many important Delawareans. At the green's other end, the 1732 **New Castle Courthouse** *(302-323-4453. Closed Mon.)* served as Delaware's colonial capitol until 1777 and now holds exhibits on state history; the old town hall is adjacent.

The town's finest manor house, the grand federal-style **Read House★** *(42 The Strand. 302-322-8411. March-Dec. Tues.-Sun., Jan.-Feb. Sat.-Sun., and by appt.; adm. fee)* overlooks the Delaware River. According to the guides, the somewhat hapless George Read, Jr., built the grandest house in town to prove he could live up to his larger-than-life father, a prominent statesman and a signer of the Declaration of Independence. Read's home includes elaborate punch-and-dart woodwork, elegant arches in the center hall, and 13-foot ceilings. A local attorney, Read did not attain the financial success necessary to support his lavish lifestyle and died in debt, forcing his heirs to sell the house and its furnishings. In the 1920s, the wealthy Lairds bought the house and began a colonial revival restoration. Today several rooms reflect their lifestyle, while the remainder of the house is decorated in early 18th-century pieces that re-create the furnishings of the Read period. The formal gardens have kept their mid-18th-century appearance.

Great Egret, Bombay Hook National Wildlife Refuge

From New Castle, follow Del. 9 several miles south to Delaware City, where a short ferry ride will take you across the Delaware River to Pea Patch Island, site of **Fort Delaware** *(Ferry dock at end of Clinton St. 302-834-7941. Ferry operates mid-June–Labor Day Wed.-Sun., May and Sept. weekends).* Now a state park, the Civil War fort is well interpreted by living history actors representing both Union men and the Confederates imprisoned here. The irregularly shaped brick fortress was part of a coastal system of fortifications planned after the War of 1812. Finally completed in 1861, the moated fort became the administrative hub of a prison camp during the Civil War. Barracks stretching across the end of the island held some

12,000 prisoners, and the total island population reached 14,000, making it the largest city in Delaware. Undergoing extensive restoration, the fort now features restored offices, kitchens, and other quarters, with original casemates and battlements still in place. A nature walk leads to wetlands rich in birdlife.

From Delaware City, Del. 9 twists south through reedy marshlands and farm fields along the Delaware River. In the crossroads of Port Penn, you can follow the boardwalked **Port Penn Wetland Trail** to explore the habitat that has meant so much to both the human and animal population of this coastal area.

At the junction with Del. 299, take a brief detour to **3 Odessa★** *(Historic Houses of Odessa, 2nd and Main Sts. 302-378-4069. March-Dec. Tues.-Sun.; adm. fee to houses).* Once a thriving commercial port, Odessa today drowses sleepily, its late 18th-century buildings seemingly untouched by time. Winterthur now owns four of the town's Main Street buildings. The **Corbit-Sharp House,** an elegant Georgian mansion built in 1772 by successful Quaker tanner William Corbit, still retains its fine woodwork and a number of original furnishings. The adjacent Georgian **Wilson-Warner House,** built in 1769 by Corbit's brother-in-law, tells a different tale. Wilson's success was short-lived, and in 1829 he was forced into bankruptcy. Today, furnishings are pushed to the side as if in preparation for the bankruptcy sale. The **Brick Hotel Gallery** functioned as a hostelry in the 19th century, but now houses a museum devoted to the ornate Victorian furnishings produced by New York craftsman, John Henry Belter. The **Collins-Sharp House** is one of the town's earliest structures, surviving from the early 1700s and now devoted to hands-on demonstrations of cooking and crafts. A number of other privately owned historic homes, many marked by plaques, edge the town's shaded streets.

Backtrack to Del. 9 and continue south. After about 10 miles, begin looking for the turnoff to **4 Bombay Hook National Wildlife Refuge** *(Whitehall Neck Rd. 302-653-6872. Visitor Center closed weekends in summer and winter; adm. fee).* Nature trails and a 12-mile driving tour through refuge lands explore the almost 16,000 acres of protected tidal saltmarsh and wooded swamplands. During spring and fall, the refuge attracts thousands of migrating waterfowl. In May and June, shorebirds concentrate here to feed off the horseshoe crab eggs that proliferate along the bayshore and in the mudflats.

Maryland Roots

Two of the 19th century's most notable African Americans were born into slavery within a couple of years and a few miles of one another. Frederick Douglass (circa 1817-1895) began life on the enormous plantation owned by Edward Lloyd that sprawled across Talbot County. Harriet Tubman (circa 1820-1913) grew up on the Brodas family's plantation in adjacent Dorchester County. Both escaped to the North as young adults, but neither forgot the plight of their fellow African Americans held in bondage in the South. Douglass became a leading figure among abolitionists and Tubman a courageous conductor on the Underground Railroad, guiding hundreds of slaves to freedom.

About 7 miles south of the refuge, the drive turns inland on Del. 8 and continues into Delaware's lovely little capital of 5 **Dover** *(Visitor Center 302-739-4266).* In 1777 the British captured the colonial capital of New Castle, forcing the legislators to flee south. They continued meeting in Dover's taverns, and the town remained the seat of state government. Massive brick colonial revival government buildings front Capitol Square, including the privately owned **Sewell C. Biggs Museum of American Art**★ *(North and Federal Sts. 302-674-2111. Wed.-Sun.),* located above the state Visitor Center. Galleries here display elegantly crafted 18th- and 19th-century silver and furniture, as well as works of art by Thomas Sully, Frank Schoonover, John Singer Sargent, and Hiram Powers.

Nearby, the town's small but historic **green** was designated as such by state founder, William Penn in 1683. It was here on December 7, 1787, in the Golden Fleece Tavern that once fronted the green, that Delaware became the "First State" to ratify the U.S. Constitution. The green is still edged by 18th- and 19th-century row houses, but its finest piece of architecture is Delaware's original **State House** *(302-739-4266. Closed Mon.).* The well-proportioned Georgian brick building has stood since 1792 and served as the legislative seat for 140 years. Restored to its 18th-century appearance in 1976, the State House is now graced by double staircases that re-create the originals and by period furnishings in the old courtroom, legislative chambers, and offices. A few blocks away, **Christ Episcopal Church** *(S. State and Water Sts. 302-734-5731)* has undergone many additions and changes since it was first sited here in 1734. Most notable among the alterations are the compelling neo-Gothic stained-glass windows added in the late 19th century.

Costumed interpreter, John Dickinson Plantation

Dover's 1790s Presbyterian Church and its 1880s Sunday school building have been converted into the **Meeting House Galleries** *(North St. and Governors Ave. 302-739-4266. Tues.-Sat.),* whose two buildings display exhibits on archaeology, Native Americans, and "Main Street,

Docked sailboat, St. Michaels, Maryland

Delaware," a re-creation of the shops found in the southern part of the state at the turn of the century. Behind the museum buildings, the **Johnson Victrola Museum** *(302-739-4266. Tues.-Sat.)* honors the foresight of Delaware native Eldridge Reeves Johnson, who in 1901 cofounded the Victor Talking Machine Company. The museum's extensive collection of old Victrola's and memorabilia of their beloved mascot, the cock-eared dog Nipper, conjures a nostalgia for the early decades of this century.

More pieces of the past are displayed at the **Delaware Agricultural Museum and Village** *(US 13. 302-734-1618. Apr.-Dec. Tues.-Sun., weekdays in winter; adm. fee).* Situated amid the noise of shopping centers and traffic, this enclave of the past re-creates a small farming town at the end of the 19th century, complete with church, barbershop, and school relocated from the surrounding countryside, including Cecile Steele's original broiler house. Her 1923 innovation led to the development of the commercial broiler industry that still thrives in her native Delaware.

Take US 13 and US 113 south to the southern outskirts of Dover, where the **John Dickinson Plantation** *(340 Kitts Hummock Rd., off US 113. 302-739-3277. March-Dec. Tues.-Sun., Jan.-Feb. Tues.-Sat.; adm. fee)* commemorates the "Penman of the American Revolution." A major formulator of the Constitution, Dickinson grew up on this plantation in the mid-1700s. In 1804 the original brick manor house burned and Dickinson rebuilt it. Today, it's filled with period antiques.

The drive follows US 113 south to Milford, then turns inland on Del. 14, threading through the rich farm country of the Delmarva Peninsula. At the Maryland town of Denton, pick up Md. 328 and follow it into 6 **Easton** *(Visitor Center, 210 Marlboro St. 410-822-4606).* Hub of tony Talbot County, Easton and its environs harbor lovely houses and old estates. The **Historical Society of Talbot County** *(25 S. Washington St. 410-822-0773. Tues.-Sun.; adm. fee)* features changing exhibits and offers tours of its adjacent historic houses. The 1810 **James Neall House** was the comfortable home of an affluent Quaker cabinetmaker, and in the garden behind it, his brother Joseph's pleasant cottage offers a view of a more modest lifestyle. For a look at the work of contemporary artists of the Eastern Shore and of American notables like James McNeil Whistler, stop by the **Academy of the Arts** *(106 South St. 410-822-0455. Mon.-Sat.; donation),* inside a converted 1820s schoolhouse.

Like much of the Delmarva Peninsula, Easton historically enjoyed a Quaker presence, one that continues at the **Third Haven Friends Meeting House** *(405 S. Washington St. 410-822-0293).* Erected in the 1680s, the simple frame building predates the town. The adjacent brick meetinghouse was built in 1880.

Leave Easton on Md. 33 as it dips west through a narrow peninsula filigreed by rivers and extending out into the Chesapeake Bay. In less than 10 miles, the drive enters **St. Michaels,** one of the most popular tourist spots on the Eastern Shore. Fronting the Miles River just off the bay, the town prospered as a shipbuilding center throughout the 18th century. Borrowing on those roots, the once quiet village became home to the **Chesapeake Bay Maritime Museum**★★ *(Mill St. 410-745-2916. Daily March-Jan., weekends in Feb.; adm. fee),* one of the country's finest maritime museums. Built in 1965, the 18-acre complex now includes eight exhibition buildings, the centerpiece being the old 1870 screwpile Hooper Strait Lighthouse. The museum traces the area's long reliance on the water, explaining the skills of the Chesapeake watermen, the crafts they use, and the way they harvest the bay's bountiful seafood. Other buildings explore the bay's natural history and the wide array of bay crafts that have plied Chesapeake waters.

Old houses from the last century face the town's narrow streets, crowded with visitors on pleasant weekends. Many ferry back and forth between here and the

Bay Bounty

Baltimore's H. L Mencken called the Chesapeake Bay "an immense protein factory," and indeed in past decades it has provided the area's traditional watermen a bountiful living off the oysters, clams, blue crabs, and fish they've harvested. However, chemical pollutants and blights (and possibly overharvesting) have recently seriously damaged the largess of this immense, shallow estuary, whose average depth is around 20 feet. Happily, conservation methods are slowly beginning to restore the bay's health, to the delight of seafood-lovers, sportfishermen, and especially the region's watermen.

nearby town of **Oxford★★.** To do so yourself, follow the signs as you leave town for the **Oxford-Bellevue Ferry** *(Landing outside St. Michaels off Md. 329. 410-745-9023. Daily June-Aug., Mon.-Sat. March-May and Sept.–mid-Dec., closed rest of year; fare),* which chugs across the Tred Avon River. The wide streets and pristine beauty of Oxford make it one of the most appealing villages along this part of the East Coast. Now an upscale haven for yachtsmen, the town became a port of entry and bustled with commerce at the end of the 1600s. The **Oxford Museum** *(Morris and Market Sts. 410-226-0191. Weekends mid-April–mid-Oct.)* showcases local memorabilia and offers walking tour maps of this attractive town. The respected **Robert Morris Inn** *(314 N. Morris St. 410-226-5111)* incorporates the home of the Revolutionary War financier into an 19th-century-style inn.

Figurehead, Chesapeake Bay Maritime Museum, St. Michaels

Return to Easton on Md. 333 and continue north on US 50 for about 20 miles, where a short detour on Md. 662 leads to the little hamlet of 7 **Wye Mills.** Here the old 17th-century gristmill *(410-827-6909. April-Nov.)* that gave the crossroads its name still stands, as does the huge 450-year-old **Wye Oak,** credited with being the oldest white oak in the country.

Leaving Wye Mills, the drive joins Md. 213 north, which leads to 8 **Chestertown** *(Kent County Chamber of Commerce, 400 S. Cross St. 410-778-0416. Driving tour maps available),* yet another lovely historic town. The Historical Society of Kent County houses its collection of local history at the **Geddes-Piper House** *(Church Alley. 410-778-3499. Wed.-Mon.; adm. fee).* Graced with other fine private houses from the 1700s, the town boasts a tree-shaded Main Street and friendly townsfolk reminiscent of kinder, gentler times.

Heading back to Wilmington via Md. 213 and US 40 (or I-95), be sure to stop at picturesque 9 **Chesapeake City,** which sits beside the Chesapeake & Delaware Canal. Completed in 1829, the canal saved ocean-going vessels a nearly 300-mile trip around the Delmarva Peninsula. The **Chesapeake & Delaware Canal Museum** *(815 Bethel Rd. 410-885-5622. Closed Sun.)* houses canal memorabilia, and the tiny, shop-filled downtown is perfect for strolling.

Coastal Loop ★★

● 215 miles ● 3 days ● Year-round

Ocean-quickened breezes and the glint of wheeling gulls are constant companions on this coastline drive. Beginning in a historic colonial community, the route moves south down the Delmarva (Delaware–Maryland–Virginia) Peninsula, a wide and wonderful tongue of land between the Atlantic Ocean and Chesapeake Bay. Along the way the drive takes in resort cities; quieter beach towns; state parks; and a national seashore, Assateague, where the ocean rolls onto broad white beaches and wild ponies graze the coastal plains. On the old waterman's island of Chincoteague, restaurants serve up local seafood and birders flock to one of the country's most popular wildlife refuges.

The drive begins at lovely little ❶ **Lewes★,** whose original Dutch name, Zwaanendael, means "valley of the swans." It seems fitting for this tidy village, which, in spite of the region's predominant beachgoing ambience, clings to its status as "the first town in the first state." You can learn how the Dutch settled here in 1631 and about the town's subsequent heyday as a colonial port at the eye-catching **Zwaanendael Museum** *(Savannah Rd. and King's Hwy. 302-645-9418. Tues.-Sat.; donation).* Modeled after a Dutch town hall, its redbrick exterior mounts to a flourish of cornices and curlicues. Next door the quaint, early 18th-century **Fisher Martin House** *(302-645-8073)* is now the town's Visitor Center.

Along the boardwalk, Rehoboth Beach

A block away is West Third Street and an old barn called the **Preservation Forge,** whose modern-day blacksmith happily explains his craft to passersby. Occupying a shady greensward, the **Lewes Historical Society Complex** *(3rd and Shipcarpenter Sts. 302-645-7670. Mid-June–Labor Day Tues.-Sat.; adm. fee)* also celebrates old traditions, with a cluster of historic cedar-shake houses, shops, and offices that re-create life in the 1800s.

The town itself lies along the Lewes and Rehoboth Canal, where sail riggings chime and the historical society allows the public a look at the 1930s lightship *Overfalls.* A few miles east, the Atlantic crashes to shore at one of the least crowded stretches of beach along this part of the coastline—**Cape Henlopen State Park★** *(E on US 9. 302-645-8983).* During World War II, much of the cape was militarized as Fort Miles, and a 70-foot-high concrete tower still stands from those days.

From the cape follow US 9 west and Del. 1 south to **Rehoboth Beach.** Here Rehoboth Avenue (US 1A) leads to a boardwalk edged by T-shirt and saltwater-taffy shops, fronting a boisterous beach filled with cadres of teens and sand-bucket-toting toddlers. By night Rehoboth offers numerous eateries and a small, old-fashioned amusement park. The town had far more sedate beginnings, as a popular place for Methodist camp meetings in the late 1800s, an era recalled by the **Rehoboth Railroad Station** *(501 Rehoboth Ave. 302-227-2233 or 800-441-1329),* now a Visitor Center.

To get a sense of Rehoboth's year-round neighborhoods, leave town on Second Avenue, weaving past the well-kept houses surrounding Silver Lake before intersecting with Del. 1 in the funky little resort community of **Dewey Beach.** Heading south, Del. 1 passes into **Delaware Seashore State Park★** *(302-227-2800),* over 2,700 acres running between the Atlantic Ocean and Rehoboth and Indian River Bays. Long, white, and lovely, these beaches offer a quieter alternative to town beaches.

Cross Indian River Inlet to **2** **Bethany Beach,** perhaps the most upscale of this string of coastal beach enclaves. Bethany considers itself a bit more dignified than the rest, with a small, low-key boardwalk and less commercialism.

Del. 1 heads through **Fenwick Island State Park** *(302-539-9060)* with views west across the open stretches of Little Assawoman Bay. The drive soon enters Maryland and the megaresort of **3** **Ocean City** *(Visitor Information 410-213-0552 or 800-OC-OCEAN).* Miles of shops, condos, hotels, seafood restaurants, and miniature golf courses vie for attention on this mini-peninsula, bordered by two large inland bays, the Atlantic, and the Inlet. But the main attraction unquestionably remains the city's wide and luxurious beach, built up in part by a jetty system capturing ocean sands. A 2.9-mile-long **boardwalk★,** extending from 27th Street south to South Division Street, effectively serves as the city's main stem; every 20 minutes in summer, trains run its length. The boardwalk's southern end is dominated by two somewhat raucous amusement parks, featuring a 104-year-old restored carousel. The red-roofed, white frame **Ocean City Life-Saving Station Museum** *(Boardwalk at the Inlet. 410-289-4991. Daily May-Oct., weekends in winter; adm. fee),* moved from its original Caroline Street location in 1977, seems a little incongruous among the boardwalk clutter. It now serves as a museum dedicated to the history of lifesaving, the destructive might of the Atlantic, and the diversity of

Ocean City boardwalk amusement park by night

the marine world. Be sure to see the intriguing little case that displays multicolored sands from beaches around the world.

Turning inland briefly, the drive crosses Isle of Wight Bay on US 50, then quickly angles south on Md. 611, rambling 7 miles through a few open farm fields toward **Assateague Island National Seashore★★** *(410-641-1441. Adm. fee).* The seashore's Barrier Island Visitor Center offers a worthwhile movie explaining the natural history of Atlantic barrier islands like Assateague, as well as a touch-tank aquarium popular with kids. From here the road crosses onto the island itself. Straight ahead lies 4 **Assateague State Park** *(410-641-2120. Adm. fee),* a small beach area bordered on both sides by the national seashore. Edging past low coastal thickets of holly and bayberry, the road heads south a few miles while the ocean hides behind a line of dunes that send streamers of sand up into the wind. Keep a look out for the wild "ponies"—actually small horses—that have made this stretch of Atlantic famous. Legend insists the horses were shipwrecked off the coast and swam ashore, but the National Park Service unromantically claims the animals descended from the livestock of 17th-century planters. While Assateague's pristine beach is a delight, it's also worth walking over to the island's inland side, where a marsh-fringed coastline overlooks serene Sinepuxent Bay. Assateague stretches a long, lazy 37 miles down the coast and into Virginia and, though the paved road quickly ends, recreational vehicles can follow the sands far down the island.

Retrace your route on Md. 611 to its intersection with Md. 376. Take this to US 113, which leads south to 5 **Snow Hill,** an elegant old river town threaded by the lazy tides of the Pocomoke River. Founded as a colonial port in 1642, the peaceful and stately settlement is now graced with gabled and verandaed Victorians, particularly along Federal Street. The **Julia A. Purnell Museum** *(208 W. Market St. 410-632-0515. April-Oct. and by appt.; adm. fee),* housed in a small late Victorian Catholic church, displays local memorabilia. Local outfitters rent canoes, some with narrated cruises, for exploring the Pocomoke's tannin-brown waters past forests darkened with pine and cypress.

Just east of a section of the Pocomoke State Forest, **Furnace Town Historic Site★** *(4 miles NW on Md. 12 to marked turnoff. 410-632-2032. April-Oct.; adm. fee)* rests beneath high pines near Nassawango Creek. One of a handful of ghost towns dotting the Atlantic coastal plain,

The Ward Brothers

They were barbers by profession, Lem and Steve Ward, with a small shop in the bay town of Crisfield. Their father died when the boys were young, and they, like most locals, hunted waterfowl for food. And like other locals, they made their own decoys, Steve carving and Lem painting them. In the 1920s, they began experimenting with their decoys, creating carvings that were more than just crude forms but actually looked like birds—and eventually like decorative works of art. By mid-century, the brothers had been "discovered" by a larger world. Though Steve died in 1976, Lem kept up their work, gaining recognition from both the governor of Maryland and President Reagan. In 1975 the fine museum that bears their name and continues their tradition opened in Salisbury, Maryland (see page 155).

this small village thrived in the early 19th century on the production of pig iron. Remains of the old brick iron furnace still rise at the edge of the 25-acre village, whose small clapboard buildings, most moved here from elsewhere, are peopled by artisans practicing such early crafts as broom-making, blacksmithing, and weaving. A mile-long Nature Conservancy trail leads through the bordering forest to a broodingly beautiful cypress swamp.

Boats docked at Chincoteague Harbor

Return to Snow Hill and continue south on Md. 12, past rural hamlets marked by plank-floored general stores. Some 8 miles after crossing into Virginia, the route intersects with Chincoteague Road (Va. 175), leading east past NASA's **Wallops Flight Facility** and onto a causeway arrowing across a superb sun-streaked tidal marsh. The causeway ends right in the heart of the old waterman's community of 6 **Chincoteague★**, where workboats rest at anchor and modest shingle houses sit in tidy yards. The town is famous for many things: its succulent salt oysters; the unforgettable accent of its locals (a kind of clipped, fast-moving Cornish patois); and its ponies, made legendary by Marguerite Henry's 1947 classic, *Misty of Chincoteague*. Every July spectators flock here to the annual penning of the area's semi-wild ponies, where local firemen round up the ponies, auctioning off the foals to an enthusiastic public.

Pony, Chincoteague National Wildlife Refuge

Chincoteague National Wildlife Refuge★★ *(Visitor Center just after bridge onto Assateague Island. 757-336-6122)* actually lies at the south end of Assateague Island and right along the Atlantic flyway. Its rich marshlands and impoundments fill with thousands of migrating shorebirds, peaking in late spring and early fall. But the refuge attracts a diverse show of birdlife year-round, from the snow geese and ducks that winter here, to the herons and egrets that stalk the shallows primarily in summer. Birding is probably best along the 3-mile **Wildlife Loop,** equally popular with bikers, hikers, and mosquitoes (cars are allowed only from 3 p.m. to dusk). Beyond the trail, the main park road leads out through the marshes to the sweeping beaches of southern Assateague. The candy-striped **Assateague Lighthouse** rises above the grassy salt marshes, flashing a warning to mariners since the 1800s. Originally built at the southern tip of the island, it now lies inland, owing to the natural buildup of the coastline.

If you're a decoy fan, stop at the **Refuge Waterfowl Museum** *(7059 Maddox Blvd. 757-336-5800. Adm. fee),* a gallery that displays early Chincoteague carvings, sells decoys, and offers a history of waterfowl hunting in these marshlands. Or just drive along island backroads and look for signs on houses announcing "decoys" or "decoy carver." Decoy carving has long been a tradition here.

Beach surf casting, Rehoboth Beach

The world's premier decoy museum lies about 50 miles northwest in the Maryland city of 7 **Salisbury.** Overlooking a wildfowl pond, the modern **Ward Museum of Wildfowl Art★★** *(909 S. Schumaker Dr. 410-742-4988. Adm. fee)* holds a superb collection of traditional decoys, many carved by the legendary Ward brothers of nearby Crisfield (see sidebar page 152). You can also view the exquisitely detailed works of art that have won the museum's annual world championship wildfowl carving competition.

Wildlife is also celebrated at the small **Salisbury Zoo** *(755 S. Park Dr. 410-548-3188)*, where paths lead past landscaped enclosures prowled by bobcats and bison, ocelots and alligators. Among Salisbury's fine old houses is an exemplar of transitional Georgian architecture, **Poplar Hill Mansion** *(117 Elizabeth St. 410-749-1776. Most Sun. afternoons and by appt.; donation)*. Begun in 1799, the brick-and-clapboard house possesses Palladian windows and large, stately rooms.

From Salisbury, US 13 and US 9 lead northeast back to Lewes, passing by roadside produce stands and some of the Eastern Shore's best farm country.

For More Information

WASHINGTON, D.C.

Washington D.C. Convention & Visitors Association *202-789-7000*. General information including touring, lodging, and restaurants.

National Park Service Information *202-619-7222*.

Smithsonian Information Center *202-357-2700*.

VIRGINIA

Virginia Tourism Corporation General information *804-786-4484* or *800-932-5827*. B&B information and reservations *202-659-5523* or *800-934-9184*.

Dept. of Conservation and Recreation General information *804-786-1712*. Cabin or camping reservations *800-933-7275*.

Dept. of Game and Inland Fisheries *804-367-1000*. Hunting and freshwater fishing licenses.

Dept. of Transportation Road conditions and special travel information *800-367-ROAD*.

Marine Resources Commission *800-541-4646*. Saltwater fishing licenses.

Shenandoah National Park *540-999-3500*. General information including camping, lodging, and Skyline Drive.

Shenandoah Valley Travel Association *800-434-5323*. Fall foliage update.

WEST VIRGINIA

West Virginia Division of Tourism *304-558-2200* or *800-CALL-WVA*. General information including recreational activities, lodging, touring, B&Bs, and fall foliage hot spots. For state park information ask for Parks and Recreation.

Department of Transportation Road conditions *304-558-3758*.

Monongahela National Forest *304-636-1800*.

Wildlife Resources *304-558-2771*. Fishing and hunting licenses.

MARYLAND

Maryland Office of Tourism General information and calendar of events *410-767-3400* or *800-MD IS FUN*. Fall foliage update and festival information 800-*LEAVES*.

Dept of Natural Resources Fishing information *800-688-FINS*. Hunting information *410-974-3195*.

State Forest and Park Service *410-974-3771* or *800-830-3974*.

State Highway Administration Road conditions *410-545-0301*.

State Highway Administration Severe Weather Hotline *800-327-3125*.

Bed & Breakfasts of Maryland *410-269-6232* or *800-736-4667*.

DELAWARE

Delaware Tourism Office *302-739-4261* or *800-441-8846*. General information and calendar of events.

Dept. of Transportation Road conditions *302-739-6677*. Interstate and turnpike information *302-368-6855*.

Division of Fish and Wildlife *302-739-4431*. Fishing and hunting licenses.

Division of Parks and Recreation *302-739-4702*.

HOTEL & MOTEL CHAINS

(Accommodations in all four states and Washington, D.C., unless otherwise noted. Though some hotels may not be in Washington, D.C., proper, they may be located nearby in Virginia or Maryland)

Best Western International *800-528-1234*

Budget Host *800-BUD HOST* (except D.C. and Del.)

Choice Hotels *800-4-CHOICE*

Clarion Hotels *800-CLARION*

Comfort Inns *800-228-5150*

Days Inn *800-325-2525*

Doubletree Hotels and Guest Suites *800-222-TREE* (except Del. and W. Va.)

Econo Lodge *800-446-6900* (except D.C.)

Embassy Suites *800-362-2779* (except Del. and W. Va.)

Fairfield Inn by Marriott *800-228-2800* (except D.C. and W. Va.)

Friendship Inns Hotel *800-453-4511* (Md. and Va. only)

Hampton Inn *800-HAMPTON* (except D.C.)

Hilton Hotels *800-HILTONS* (except W. Va.)

Holiday Inns *800-HOLIDAY*

Howard Johnson *800-654-2000*

Hyatt Hotels & Resorts 800-233-1234 (except Del. and W. Va.)

LRI Loews Hotels *800-223-0888* (D.C. and Md. only)

Motel 6 *800-466-8356* (except D.C.)

Quality Inns-Hotels-Suites *800-228-5151* (except W. Va.)

Radisson Hotels International *800-333-3333*

Ramada Inns *800-2-RAMADA* (except D.C.)

Red Roof Inns *800-843-7663* (except D.C.)

Ritz-Carlton *800-241-3333* (D.C. and Va. only)

Sheraton Hotels & Inns *800-325-3535* (except W. Va.)

Super 8 Motels *800-843-1991*

Travelodge Intl., Inc. *800-255-3050* (except Md.)

Utell International *800-223-9868*

Westin Hotels and Resorts *800-228-3000* (D.C. only)

Wyndham Hotels and Resorts *800-822-4200* (D.C. and Md. only)

Index

ILLUSTRATIONS CREDITS

Cover Photo: Ken Sherman/Graphistock

Pete Souza photographed Washington, D.C., Maryland, and Delaware except for the following: 24 Martin Rogers; 25 Richard Nowitz/NGS Image Collection; 38 Sisse Brimberg, National Geographic Photographer; 48 James P. Blair; 49 Gail Mooney; 126-127 (both) Sam Abell, National Geographic Photographer; 136 George Grall; 137 Annie Griffiths Belt; 153 (upper) Richard Nowitz.

Richard Nowitz photographed Virginia and West Virginia except for the following: 51-58 (all) Pete Souza; 98 Richard A. Cooke, III.

The sculpture in the photograph on page 28, photographed by Pete Souza, is identified as follows: Paul Manship, "Dancer and Gazelles" 1916 bronze. 693/4 x 73 x 19". In the Collection of The Corcoran Gallery of Art, Washington, D.C. Museum purchase, 1920.

NOTES ON AUTHOR AND PHOTOGRAPHERS

K. M. KOSTYAL has written for National Geographic publications for almost 20 years. A contributing editor to NATIONAL GEOGRAPHIC TRAVELER, she has covered destinations ranging from Europe to the Antarctic. Her most recent work for the Society, *Field of Battle: The Civil War Letters of Maj. Thomas Halsey,* was published in 1996. She lives in Alexandria, Virginia, with her husband, Buzz Smith, and son, Will.

RICHARD NOWITZ was named 1996 Travel Photographer of the Year by the Society of American Travel Writers (SATW) and has been a National Geographic contract photographer since 1992 with WORLD magazine, the Society's children's publication. Nowitz has been the principal photographer of over 11 large format books and travel guides of destinations around the world. He has contributed to other National Geographic Society book projects and is represented by the NGS Image Collection.

A native of South Dartmouth, Massachusetts, freelance photographer PETE SOUZA has lived in Arlington, Virginia, for the past 13 years. He is a frequent contributor to the National Geographic Society and has photographed two articles for NATIONAL GEOGRAPHIC magazine. Souza has won numerous photojournalism awards, including this year a first and second place in the prestigious Pictures of the Year competition for his coverage of the Million Man March in Washington, D.C. In 1992 Souza produced and published *Unguarded Moments: Behind-the-Scenes Photographs of President Reagan,* a large format book based on his 51/2 years as official White House photographer.

Composition for this book by the National Geographic Society Book Division. Printed and bound by R.R. Donnelly & Sons, Willard, Ohio. Color separations by Digital Color Image, Pensauken, New Jersey. Paper by Consolidated/Alling & Cory, Willow Grove, Pennsylvania. Cover printed by Miken Companies, Inc. Cheektowaga, New York.

Library of Congress Cataloging-in-Publication Data

Kostyal, K. M., 1951-
National Geographic's driving guides to America. Washington, D.C. / by K.M. Kostyal; ; photographed by Richard Nowitz and Pete Souza ; prepared by the Book Division, National Geographic Society.
p. cm.
Includes index.
ISBN 0-7922-3426-X
1. Washington (D.C.)--Tours. 2. Automobile travel--Washington (D.C.)—Guidebooks. 3. Washington Region—Tours. 4. Automobile travel—Washington Region—Guidebooks. I. Nowitz, Richard. II. Souza, Pete. II. National Geographic Society (U.S.). Book Division. III. Title.
F192.3.K69 1996
917.5304'4--dc20 96-41239
CIP

Visit the Society's Web site at http://www.nationalgeographic.com or GO NATIONAL GEOGRAPHIC on CompuServe.